LIVING
WITH LOSS

Also by Ellen Sue Stern

QUANTITY SALES

Most Dell books are available at special quantity discounts when purchased in bulk by corporations, organizations, or groups. Special imprints, messages, and excerpts can be produced to meet your needs. For more information, write to: Dell Publishing, 1540 Broadway, New York, NY 10036. Attention: Special Markets.

INDIVIDUAL SALES

Are there any Dell books you want but cannot find in your local stores? If so, you can order them directly from us. You can get any Dell book currently in print. For a complete up-to-date listing of our books and information on how to order, write to: Dell Readers Service, Box DR, 1540 Broadway, New York, NY 10036.

LIVING WITH LOSS

ELLEN SUE STERN

A DELL TRADE PAPERBACK

A DELL TRADE PAPERBACK

Published by
Dell Publishing
a division of
Bantam Doubleday Dell Publishing Group, Inc.
1540 Broadway
New York, New York 10036

Library of Congress Cataloging in Publication Data
Stern, Ellen Sue, 1954–
    Living with loss : meditations for grieving widows / Ellen Sue Stern.
        p.   cm. — (Days of healing, days of change)
    ISBN 0-440-50598-4
    1. Widows—Religious life—Meditations. 2. Widows—Conduct of
life. 3. Devotional calendars. I. Title. II. Series.
BL625.7.S73   1995
155.9′37—dc20   94-45428
                                                                      CIP

Printed in the United States of America

Published simultaneously in Canada

August 1995

10 9 8 7 6 5 4 3 2 1

FFG

To my friend and mother-in-law
Jane Stern—who is a shining example of
the sort of woman
I hope to become someday

ACKNOWLEDGMENTS

Writing this book truly required the insight and experience of women who were kind and courageous enough to openly share their stories of loss. I thank all of you for helping me understand your unique struggles.

I also want to thank my children, Zoe and Evan, who gave up the end of their summer vacation with Mom so that I could complete this project. My gratitude to Wes Keye, for your gracious financial support, Steven Kaplan, for coming through for me again and again, Jill Edelstein, my dear, dear friend, and Betsy Bundschuh, for pushing me to give my best.

INTRODUCTION

I must admit that I was hesitant to write this book. For the first time in my career, I was writing about a topic I thankfully had no personal experience with; besides, I frankly expected the subject of widowhood to be morbid and depressing.

I was wrong on both counts. The further I delved into this material, the more I realized how universal the themes of loss and change really are. Although I haven't experienced the death of a loved one, I have certainly suffered the pain of losing a spouse through divorce; the themes of grief, denial, rage, acceptance, and the ongoing challenge to rebuild one's life have been recurring struggles that so many of us have grappled with in our own way. This is why I have alternatively used the terms "I," "we," and "you" when appropriate throughout the text. I have chosen to use "I" in those places where I genuinely felt a personal connection, with all due respect for the reality that in some ways this is a life stage I have yet to go through.

I was also surprised to discover that the journey through widowhood isn't all grim; in fact, there are positive aspects: increased freedom and independence, the chance to rediscover our identity and update our choices, the opportunity to form new relationships, as well as the enriched spiritual sense of purpose and meaning that comes from having faced death and courageously picked up the pieces of our lives.

None of this is to diminish the pain of losing one's spouse. However, as in all experiences of grief and healing, the opportunity for personal growth is part and parcel of having suffered and pushed through the pain. Which is why this book includes passages that are positive, hopeful, and humorous as well as numerous entries that reflect the unspeakable sorrow and mourning that widows share. I have tried to let the painful issues be painful, without sugar-coating them in any way. Likewise, I have offered some degree of optimism —a ray of light—that hopefully will sustain in times of darkness.

Throughout these pages there are several "survival checklist" items which pertain to practical considerations of widowhood. These are tangible tasks to attend to; recommendations (not assignments!) based on the experience of hundreds of widows.

If there is one truth I've learned from the widows who helped me in writing this book, it's this: Life gets better. It takes time. It occurs gradually. Each day gets a little easier, and I hope this book does its part in smoothing the way.

Two by two, marching into the ark, I said to myself as I watched the rest of the world go by.

—XENIA ROSE

Suddenly the world seems painfully coupled. Everyone seems part of a pair: couples holding hands, lingering over a candlelit dinner, sharing popcorn at the movies, evoke bittersweet memories and a fair share of envy and longing.

The prospect of going out solo can be daunting: we feel acutely aware of our single status, which intensifies our feelings of loss. But we can't remain home forever. Little by little, we need to venture out into the world. Taking a book or a journal along is one way to ease discomfort. Seeking out other singles is another way to alter our ''Noah's Ark'' view of the world; many communities, churches, and synagogues offer singles programs specifically for the purpose of meeting others who are in the same boat.

It's not easy to take the first step, but each time it gets easier. Besides, we may meet lots of interesting people who will enrich our life.

AFFIRMATION: I am not part of a minority.

I will not forget you. I have carved you on the palm of my hand.

—ISAIAH 49:15

The truest words of all:

I will not forget you. You are in my waking thoughts, my sweetest memories, my dearest dreams.

I will not forget you. You have touched my soul, opened my eyes, changed my very experience of the universe.

I will not forget you. I see you in the flowers, the sunset, the sweep of the horizon and all things that stretch to infinity.

I will not forget you. I have carved you on the palm of my hand. I carry you with me forever.

AFFIRMATION: For every season, always.

I fired God that day.

—STEPHANIE ERICCSON

"Inside, I hear a voice that tells me I will understand how your dying fits into a greater scheme of things," writes Ericcson in her memoir, *Companion Through the Darkness,* "but even four months later, I still stubbornly think God is a bumbling idiot."

It's natural to lose faith in the face of disaster: What sort of heavenly power could have allowed, much less authored, such a senseless tragedy? But even as we question God—we should and we must—we also seek deeper understanding. The irony is that at the moment we most need spiritual sustenance, we find it most elusive.

Ultimately faith may be either dashed or strengthened. But either way it's just fine to vent anger at God. As the saying goes, "Just because you give up on God, it doesn't mean God gives up on you."

AFFIRMATION: Even if you temporarily give up . . .

The first days. People keep coming into the apartment, carrying boxes of cakes and cookies. To sweeten the taste of death?

—ANNE HOSANSKY

Face it—in the early days of mourning, most offers of comfort and solace fall short of what we need. And that's because what we need above all else—time—isn't something anyone can give.

And so our loved ones give what they can. Nourishment in the form of casseroles and coffee cakes, which we can barely nibble at without feeling as if we'll choke. "Eat, you need your strength," we hear over and over, as if blueberry muffins will heal our broken heart.

There's no sweetening the taste of death, no lessening our pain through culinary concoctions. We may even feel angered by the constant partylike atmosphere following the funeral and over the next few days when company continues to arrive.

The company of loved ones can be a blessing; it can also be exhausting and overwhelming in the midst of our grief. When you've had enough, excuse yourself. And for every gesture, say thank you, with appreciation for all the love in your life.

AFFIRMATION: I know they mean well.

I felt nothing. It was almost as if I'd been replaced by a robot that had been programmed to cope.
                                                          —DR. JOYCE BROTHERS

Numbness is nature's way of helping us remain functional in the early stages of mourning. Many widows say they "felt nothing" in the beginning but shock, a sense of unreality, being in a trancelike state in which they coped on autopilot.

And thank goodness. In the first days following our mate's death we are inundated with details; if we were to experience even a fraction of the pain, we might find it impossible to get through the funeral, not to mention maintaining our routine responsibilities.

Little by little it sinks in. At first we feel nothing, because that's what we can afford to feel. Later, as we become stronger, we can stand more pain. And more pain. Until gradually we grow a new layer of skin.

AFFIRMATION: I will feel it when I'm ready to feel it.

MONTH ONE   **DAY SIX**

*I tell widows when someone offers to help, take them up
on it. "Sure you can pick up my laundry on Thursday.
My car is out of commission."*

— LYNN CAINE

It's one sure way to weed out who's giving lip service and
who's sincere about offers of help.

It's similar to having a baby; lots of people say, "Call if
you need anything," but, when push comes to shove, are too
busy to deliver. Lots of people drop by to google at the baby,
but how many call first from the supermarket to get your list
or straighten up the house while you nurse?

Of course it's not up to anyone to read your mind. We
need to be assertive, to take the risk of spelling out specifically what we need. It's hard: we don't want to seem demanding and we aren't sure we have the strength to face
even the slightest rejection. So choose carefully whom you
ask and for what. Remember: They offered. Helping is a
tangible way for people to show their love and support.

**AFFIRMATION: I will let my loved ones be there for
me.**

*I was furious that he hadn't stopped smoking, even after
I'd begged him to.*

—PHILOMENE GATES

This may be one of the most infuriating aspects of widowhood. We feel abandoned and, goddammit, it *didn't* have to
happen!

If our spouse died of a relatively preventable illness—even
minimally—we may be consumed with anger without a release. After all, what's the point of railing at the dead?

But our rage is justified. After two angioplasties, *how*
could he have been so stupid as to ignore our pleas to watch
his fat intake and to get some exercise? Once he was diagnosed with diabetes, we begged him to cut out sugar—we
kept the fridge stocked with fresh fruit and made special
sugar-free brownies yet still he ate sugar, often in front of
our family and friends, while we stood by helplessly, not
wanting to embarrass him, yet knowing he was killing himself.

Nothing makes us feel more helpless than watching someone we love engaged in self-destructive behavior. In this case
it may have been lethal, and it's difficult to forgive him.

Take your time. Be as angry as you have to be until the
day comes when your compassion exceeds your rage, when
you can honestly say:

**AFFIRMATION: I forgive him for being a flawed hu-
man being.**

We need courage to throw away old garments which have had their day.

—FRIDJOF NANSEN

In this case it's far more than metaphor. We are faced with the actual—and often heartbreaking—task of disposing of our spouse's personal belongings. Removing and/or giving away his clothing represents yet another bit of closure— another way of letting go of the past.

Some widows get this over with right away; some wait for weeks before emptying drawers and cleaning closets; still others find it impossible to part with such intimate reminders of their beloved, leaving everything just as it was, finding comfort in being able to hold on to any and all remnants.

There is no right time, no need to feel pressured by anyone else's timetable. When you *are* ready, here are a few helpful hints from other widows: Ask a friend to be with you if that will make it easier. Give yourself several hours, so that you can relive the memories each garment evokes. And, if it seems right, pass on some chosen pieces to special friends as a way of honoring them.

Be sure to keep something for yourself. Wrapping yourself in his big flannel robe with its lingering scent of Old Spice, wearing his wristwatch, his favorite denim workshirt, his wool socks to bed, are all wonderful ways of keeping him close to your heart.

AFFIRMATION: Everything in its own good time.

Have You Decided What to Do with Your Husband's Belongings?

Sooner or later we have to deal with his clothing, correspondence, and other personal belongings. This usually occurs in three stages: First we allow ourselves to think about it. Next we force ourselves to look through his things. Third, when we're ready, we tackle this emotional project, taking time and care to disperse what he's left behind in whatever ways are most comfortable for ourselves.

What stage of this process are you in? Do what's right for what you're presently feeling.

IDENTITY

What do you call yourself? Are you still Mrs. So-and-So, your husband's name, or Mrs. Your Name?

—XENIA ROSE

It's more than semantics. For the majority of widows who took their husband's name in marriage, the "name question" is a disturbing dilemma. What we call ourselves, how we introduce ourselves in the world, reflects our deepest, most primary sense of who we are.

And who we are is changing and will continue to change over the next weeks and months as we gradually evolve into the person we are becoming. Some days we feel most comfortable and secure being Mrs. So-and-So, assuming that our spouse's name is a way of remaining symbolically connected and committed to his memory. Gradually it may feel more natural and appropriate to drop the *Mrs.* as a way of affirming our emerging status as a single person. And we may vacillate, claiming our marital moniker when it serves us. (Unfortunately widows often find their "unmarried status" a liability; many women use *Mrs.* as a way of avoiding being manipulated, overcharged, or underestimated by opportunistic individuals.)

There are no rules, no Miss Manners decorum to guide us through this decision. If being Mrs. So-and-So intensifies feelings of loss, then it may be time to rename ourselves as a way of moving on. On the other hand relinquishing his name may feel like betrayal, a sign that the time isn't right.

Only you will know if and when you're ready. No rush. For now try different names on for size to see what fits.

AFFIRMATION: A rose is a rose is a rose.

I saw that nothing was permanent.

—YOKO ONO

This is one of the hardest things of all to accept. And yet once we come to terms with life's impermanence, we are both freer to love and more able to let go.

For Yoko Ono, John Lennon's widow, lover, and soul mate, loss came at a relatively young age. At forty-seven she learned—as we all eventually learn—that no matter how intense our passion, how committed our love, our time together is as fleeting as a butterfly's wing.

Which makes what we had all the more precious. There is no time to waste. We must live fully and love passionately in the present—in the moment—which is truly all we have.

AFFIRMATION: I have come to appreciate the fragility of life.

Putting our feelings into writing is one way of remaining connected to our spouse. The process of expressing feelings, sharing news and information, asking questions, and seeking answers helps us be active agents in our own healing.

These letters will also serve as a valuable record to read and reread when you're ready. Keep them safe, they are a living history of this unique period of life.

Remember, don't censor anything. This is your chance to get it all out, in whatever words you have. Here's the first:

My Dearest_____,

I want to tell you all the things I miss about you: . . .

I fell down on the earth and spread the flowers all
around; they were like tears and they fell everywhere.
                                              —ALLIE LIGHT

With a fountain of tears we water the soil in which our
beloved rests. With beautiful flowers—symbolizing life,
growth, and continuity—we blanket his bed, connecting him
with nature, to which he has returned.

Bringing flowers to the cemetery is an act of healing and
celebration. We choose carefully—roses, lilies, the raspberry
begonias he lovingly tended in the garden—to find the perfect way to honor his spirit. Each time, we are reminded of
other floral arrangments: our wedding bouquet, roses on
Valentine's Day, the two dozen daisies he brought to the
hospital when our baby was born.

So now we come bearing flowers. It is an offering of tears.
An offering of hope. An offering of love.

AFFIRMATION: I bring you flowers.

LETTING GO

Him that I love, I wish to be free, even from me.
—ANNE MORROW LINDBERGH

Letting go is the final act of love.

It takes time, often weeks and months beyond the funeral and burial before we're fully able to relinquish our hold. It is incredibly excruciating to release our beloved. Even as we know we must, we struggle to maintain ties, clutching our pain, our memories, even our rage—all are ways of staving off the final separation that feels like a rip down the center of our heart.

Yet, little by little, we allow him to depart, to move on, yes, even to leave us, which is the greatest testimony to our love. We grant him his freedom and give him this blessing:

AFFIRMATION: Go in peace.

MONTH ONE **DAY FIFTEEN**

*We miss and need and pine for our dead, but we also
are angry at them for having abandoned us.*

—JUDITH VIORST

And we *do* feel abandoned! Although we said, "Till death do
us part," we most likely never believed we would be separated from our mate. We had so many plans together; how
dare he leave in the middle of the second or third act?

But he has. And of course we rail at the injustice. It's
called missing him—and it hurts. Nothing fills the gap; it's
him we want and we're furious that he's gone away.

Rationally we know better. The last thing he wanted was
to leave us—we may have watched him fight a brutal battle
to hang on to the bitter end.

But feelings aren't rational, and we may feel angry for a
while. It's hard to be mad at someone who is dead, but the
sooner we release our rage, the sooner we'll be able to
forgive and go on.

AFFIRMATION: I'm angry at you for leaving me!

> *The waitress says, "You can't have a booth if you're alone." I want to kill her.*
>
> —ANNE HOSANSKY

As if it wasn't hard enough to push ourselves out the door, walk into a restaurant, and say, "Table for one," we're forced to put up with rude and degrading comments that make us feel more invisible and alone.

Murder isn't an option, throwing a tantrum will humiliate us further, and walking out makes us feel like we're admitting defeat.

Don't let 'em scare you. Stand up straight, take a deep breath, and say, "I really want to sit in a booth. Is there some way that can be arranged?" If the answer is yes, great. Sometimes polite perseverance yields results. If the answer is no, do your best not to take it personally. Although it feels like an affront, it may simply be restaurant policy, based on economic concerns.

Which needn't make you feel like a second-class citizen. You can take this in stride, enjoy your meal, and make it a project to find other restaurants where you feel more welcome and at home.

AFFIRMATION: I won't be intimidated by anyone.

*I wasn't allowed to speak while my husband was alive,
and since he's gone no one has been able to shut me up.*
— HEDDA HOPPER

Although I hope this is a slight exaggeration, I suspect Hedda
Hopper isn't alone in relishing her newfound freedom to
speak her mind.

Even for those of us who were in "equal" marriages, in
which we were encouraged to express ourselves, it *is* liberat-
ing not to worry about taking center stage or fighting to
express our opinions. In fact we may find ourselves in the
position of *having* to speak up in order to get what we want,
which is another way in which widowhood forces us to become stronger and more assertive. If we often acquiesced to
our husband, it's a welcome change to find our own voice
and figure out what we as individuals think and feel, without
worrying about censoring ourselves.

This takes some getting used to. We hear our spouse's
words ringing in our ears; we may even wait for him to
correct, disagree, or debate us. Eventually we become comfortable expressing our own, unique point of view.

AFFIRMATION: I have a lot to say.

MONTH ONE   **DAY EIGHTEEN**

There was only one thing we had in common: none of us wanted to be there.

—XENIA ROSE

It's a good start! And the same could be said for almost every support group. Whether it's Alcoholics Anonymous, Living with Cancer, or a widowhood bereavement group, none of us would have eagerly signed up for membership in this particular club.

Yet it can be a real lifesaver. Some of us seize the opportunity to attend a support group, grateful for the empathy and compassion that only comes from having "been there" —a quality even the most devoted friends can't necessarily offer. On the other hand we may be put off by the idea of spilling our guts out to utter strangers, much less being burdened by their grief.

It's a personal choice with some very tangible benefits: It's a great place to meet other people who can relate to what we're going through. It's a way of learning coping strategies direct from the front lines. And it's a way of getting perspective. As we witness others in various stages of grieving, we are more able to assess our own growth and healing.

AFFIRMATION: I need and deserve support.

Have You Attended
a Grief Support Group?

Many, many women have resisted this idea, only to find it extremely helpful once they tried it. It's not for everyone—some people value privacy above all else—but there's great value in sharing common experience with others who are in some stage of bereavement.

If you're willing to take this step, contact your local hospital, religious institution, or community service agency for the closest, most convenient group. It's worth at least one visit. And by the way, you needn't say a thing. Just listening can also be healing.

Support from others has contributed so much to our healing. We wish we could tell our mate about all the help, empathy, and compassion we've received from our friends and/or from members of the grief group we attend.

Go ahead. In the following space compose a letter to your love, letting him know to whom you've turned for comfort in the wake of his death, beginning with these words:

My Dearest_____,

I didn't have any really normal minutes during those two years. It wasn't just grief. It was total confusion.
—HELEN HAYES

Forget normal. Our regular routines, along with our overall worldview, are turned topsy-turvy as we struggle for equilibrium.

We make this task more difficult by trying to get things to return to "normal"; attempts at recovering our "old life" in its familiar form only make us more frustrated and angry.

Better to throw it all to the wind. To understand and accept that we are in the throes of a transition in which it's natural to feel disoriented, lost, and confused. Life will eventually find its new order. We will settle into different routines, begin to define a new identity, crystallize a different way of life, little by little, as the dust settles.

AFFIRMATION: This is normal.

Who has words at the right moment?
—CHARLOTTE BRONTË

Our friends stumble in their effort to reach out and comfort us. They say, "I know how you feel," "I understand how hard this is for you," "I'm here if you need me." All of which leaves us angry, resentful, and lonelier, for they can't possibly know how we feel. They have no idea how hard this really is, and what we need no one else can give us.

And then there are the well-meaning, yet insensitive, comments that make us want to scream, "Shut up!" Comments such as, "At least he's out of pain," "Be glad you had so many years together," and "I'm sure you'll find someone else."

We can react—becoming incensed and outraged at these comments, which is energy draining in and of itself. *Or* we can simply say to ourselves:

AFFIRMATION: My friends are giving in the only way they know.

Preserve your memories. They're all that's left you.
                                                  —PAUL SIMON

Collecting your memories and compiling them in a photograph album will help mend your heart.

Put aside an entire afternoon so that you can spend time with each photograph: feeding him mouthfuls of wedding cake; his putting your daughter on the kindergarten bus; the one taken by the couple from Iowa you met on the cruise to the Bahamas on the last day of your vacation. And as you hold each photograph in your hand, allow the memories to wash over you. Allow yourself to smile, to weep, to feel your joy and your sadness for all the memorable times you shared.

Another, more "modern" way to maintain a living history is through videos. One woman captured the final weeks of her dying husband's life with her camcorder, which she carried with her to the hospice. "It took four months until I was ready to watch it," she says. "And though it was painful, I was eternally grateful to be able to see his face and hear him say, 'I love you.'"

It may take a few months before you're ready, but when you are, you'll find that a scrapbook or video is one more way of keeping his blessed memory alive.

AFFIRMATION: One of my fondest memories of you is . . .

HEALING

The scars on our hearts do not last forever.
— MARIANNE WILLIAMSON

Sometimes it seems as if we will never stop hurting. Are we doomed to live with a persistent ache in our heart, an empty whole in the very center of our being?

Yes and no. As New Age guru Marianne Williamson says, the scars eventually fade. We will never be the same; our scars remain, like the "battle scars" of childbirth, testimony to the intensity of our love.

But as the immediacy of our loss lessens, the sharp, throbbing pain gradually recedes to a dull ache. As we heal, there are more and more good days—days when our feelings of joy and peace exceed our grief and sorrow. Days when hopefulness exceeds despair. When gratitude exists side by side with grief.

AFFIRMATION: My scars are slowly healing.

MONTH ONE   **DAY TWENTY-FIVE**

Memory is more indelible than ink.

—ANITA LOOS

Nothing can erase our memories; they are in permanent marker, forever engraved, easily accessible when we wish to be reunited with our mate.

Yet ink is another way of preserving our memories. This is a wonderful time to keep a journal. Write in it daily; use it to record your memories of your marriage, your experiences of your spouse's death, funeral, and the days that have followed, as well as your feelings about all you're going through.

Expressing ourselves in writing is healing and empowering. A famous quote goes, "I am writing myself into well-being," and women often find it to be true. Keeping a journal is a way of naming and affirming our experience. And it is a way of measuring growth. Going back and rereading entries from last week, three months ago, three years ago, helps us see how far we've come.

AFFIRMATION: I will record my memories.

When he left me I was a middle-aged housewife. Now I am an adolescent widow, emotionally volcanic like all adolescents.

—JOAN GOULD

Mood swings. We find ourselves riding an emotional roller coaster—one minute fine, the next, feeling like a wreck.

It simply goes with the territory. We had achieved a certain degree of stability and order; our day-to-day routines were fairly set, we knew who we were, what to expect, and where we were going.

Now our lives have been thrown into chaos; our routines are disturbed, we may even experience an "identity crisis" as we navigate this new, unfamiliar terrain.

While it may feel as if you're regressing, in fact you've come a long way from adolescence. Call on your maturity, your wisdom, your perspective to guide you through this tumultuous transition.

AFFIRMATION: I am on the brink of something new.

You know you're healing when you get a phone call asking for him and you're able to say, "He's dead."
—ANNE HOSANSKY

There's something macabre about receiving phone calls from people who ask for our late spouse. Each time, it forces us to admit—again—that he's gone, and we need to figure out how to communicate this fact.

At first our words may spill out in angry torrents; we feel invaded by having to expose our very private wound. Our sadness is reactivated each time we are required to respond with some version of "He's dead" and there's little way to soften the words.

They may always hurt, but with time they will be easier to say. Like anything else, we get used to fielding phone calls and responding with the truth. Eventually the calls are fewer and farther apart until finally we no longer have to face this difficult task.

AFFIRMATION: I'll get an answering machine and screen my calls.

DOUBT

While you were alive, did I love you enough?
—ALL WIDOWS

It's the universal question widows ask themselves.

We may be plagued by doubts, lying awake at night berating ourselves for all the ways in which we could have been more giving, more patient, more loving when there was still time.

Others may feel utterly peaceful in the knowledge that what we gave was sufficient. We know we did our best; between human beings there is no perfect love, only two individuals making their best stab at life's most challenging endeavor.

The truth is, we loved him as well as we could. And that's all there is; we have to forgive ourselves for the ways in which we failed to live up to our own standards. And rest assured that our love was more than enough.

AFFIRMATION: I gave you my best.

It is never too late to ask forgiveness: for the times we took him for granted or forgot to tell him how much we loved him. For moments of thoughtlessness or neglect. For any slights, however trivial or serious, that are still hanging heavily over us now that he's gone.

Making amends doesn't depend on the actual presence of the injured party. It's enough just to say we're sorry, as long as we're absolutely sincere.

Take time now to unburden yourself. You might begin with the words:

My Dearest_____,

   I'm sorry for . . .

COMPASSION

*People who have suffered understand suffering and there-
fore extend their hand.*

—PATTI SMITH

Herein lies one of the silver linings of widowhood; our experience fills us with compassion for other people's suffering.
We are softer, more tolerant, more able to reach out to
others in need.

However, this transformation doesn't occur automatically.
If we are embittered, wallowing in anger at our misfortune,
we build a wall around ourselves that's impossible to pene-
trate. When we see our pain as universal—linking us to the
rest of humanity—our experience, however excruciating,
becomes a gift. We have been there. We know how it feels.
We want to ease the pain of all people, everywhere.

**AFFIRMATION: My suffering is making me more hu-
mane.**

*He had seen Death coming and had stood his ground
and fought it . . . to the last breath.*
—ZORA NEALE HURSTON

Another vivid memory we may be haunted by—watching
our mate fight like hell, waging a persistent battle to fight off
death's call. Some let go easily, drifting gently away; others
hang on with the last ounce of energy, every labored breath
an act of incredible willpower and determination.

We may never know what he was thinking or feeling as he
took his last breath, but we know we were privileged to
witness it. Whether he was ready to pass on or whether he
desperately clung to his life, his heroism fills us with admira-
tion.

AFFIRMATION: He was a fighter to the end.

Behind her thin black veil we saw that same face, not contorted in pain, but mask-like, frozen, still.
                              —DR. ALLA RENEE BOZARTH

This harsh assessment of the late Jackie Kennedy's composure at the funeral of her husband, President John F. Kennedy, is the first time I've ever heard anyone criticize what was widely considered impeccable grace under pressure.

But Alla Renee Bozarth has a legitimate point: Our collective perception of the most public widow of our time left an indelible mark and made a lasting statement about the value of maintaining a cool facade under the most emotionally wrenching of circumstances.

Perhaps we need to remember that behind the mask stood an intensely private woman forced to mourn before the eyes of millions. At times we, too, maintain a facade—when we're feeling self-protective or when we'd simply rather keep it together until we're home, safe and sound, where we're free to grieve in peace.

AFFIRMATION: I'm entitled to my privacy.

It is such a secret place, the land of tears.
                              —ANTOINE DE SAINT-EXUPÉRY

Sometimes we can let others hold and comfort us; other times we need absolute privacy to grieve. Our tears are the most personal expression of our pain. We release them in the safety of our bedroom, curled up in our favorite rocking chair, outdoors at the cemetery, our tears hurled against the wind, weeping to the heavens, resting against the sturdy oak tree, knowing it is strong enough to sustain us.

And then there are times when tears will only come within the tenderness of human embrace. Letting others witness our weeping is a privilege and an act of ultimate trust. It is a way of saying:

AFFIRMATION: I invite you into the secret recesses of my heart.

You can prepare for death but you can't grieve in advance.

—RABBI HOWARD JAFFE

We may have thought we were ready, emotionally prepared for our mate's death.

But as Rabbi Howard Jaffe explained following my late father-in-law, Lester's, death, we can be aware that time is running out, we can imagine the funeral, envision the emptiness, even seek bereavement counseling, but the real business of mourning can only begin with our loss.

There's a good reason for this: No matter how sick our mate was preceding death, no matter how much we intellectually knew the end was near, a part of us still clung to hope. Our grief marks the end of that hope, which is the first step toward acceptance, which ultimately, will free us from pain.

AFFIRMATION: The time to grieve is now.

Once the patient dies, I find it cruel and inappropriate to speak of the love of God.

—ELISABETH KÜBLER-ROSS

Elisabeth Kübler-Ross's definitive work, *On Death and Dying,* has much to teach us about the stages of grief and the most sensitive ways of assisting the bereaved.

Here she addresses one of the most common mistakes made in attempts to comfort widows—bringing up God's love at a time when we are wracked with doubt and when faith is at an all time low. Some of us may be reassured by comments such as "Now he's in God's hands," while others resent these words as an effort to diminish or simplify our grief. Even if we know—in our hearts—that our mate's death was destined, we may not be ready to hear it.

Remember, offers of spiritual consolation are others' attempts at reaching out. Accept them as awkward—but well-meaning—gifts.

AFFIRMATION: Don't talk to me about God right now.

Marriage resembles a pair of shears . . . always punishing anyone who comes between them.

—SYDNEY SMITH

Another serious loss—the unconditional loyalty we gave our mate and received in return.

This was one of the most wonderful aspects of marriage; we knew, regardless of our differences, that we could count on our husband to stand up for us in the face of criticism. Back home we may have duked it out, but in public we felt secure in his undying loyalty.

This may be especially keenly missed when it comes to our parenting. No matter how we felt, when it came to arguments between my grandmother and her daughters, my Papa Phillip always said, "Your mother can do no wrong." After his death she regularly invoked his memory, as if simply mentioning his name settled the case.

Now we are challenged to stand up for ourselves, and to stay close to relatives and friends who will fiercely defend us.

AFFIRMATION: Stand by me.

It was enough just to sit there without words.
                                        —LOUISE ERDRICH

No matter how wide our circle of friends, there's no replacing the quiet comfort and easy familiarity we enjoyed with our mate. What a luxury to be in the same room without speaking, one watching television, the other reading, an occasional smile to reaffirm our love and connection. The knowing glances at a dinner party, the shared pride when our child did something wondrous, the absolute security in knowing we understood each other without so much as a word, were priceless gifts that took years to develop.

This is one loss we feel sharply, especially in those awkward moments when we feel uncomfortably compelled to make small talk in social situations. When this happens, we may find ourselves easily exhausted, eager for solitude and silence. Sometimes we simply need to go home and be with ourselves and our thoughts.

AFFIRMATION: I can only put out so much energy right now.

No matter how many times you hear the word final, *it means nothing until final is actually final.*

— RUTH COUGHLIN

The finality of death is incomprehensible to anticipate, yet all too real when it ultimately comes to pass.

Until we are faced with the absolute, irrevocable ending, we are still making deals with God, bargaining for one more day, one more hour to have together. Denial is an essential coping mechanism; before, we needed our energy to comfort him, to put our affairs in order, to get through the funeral and following days. Now there is no way of escaping reality. Like the slam of a prison door, it is all too real, all too finite, as we grasp the truth, that our loss is for real, forever.

AFFIRMATION: Death is final. Love is eternal.

She knew and he knew, but neither had the courage to share it with the other. . . . and this after thirty years of marriage!

—ELISABETH KÜBLER-ROSS

We may regret not having been candid enough with our mate about his impending death. Perhaps we felt it was morbid to talk about death, that bringing it up would depress him or defeat his will to live. We may have felt obligated to remain "up" and cheerful, fearful of burdening him with our pain.

In the process we may have lost the opportunity to honestly share our feelings and comfort one another. We may each have suffered in silence, censoring our fears in an effort to protect the other.

We can't turn back time. But we *can* take comfort in knowing that:

AFFIRMATION: With words and in the comfort of silence, I was right by his side.

No one gives a funeral for the loss of hope.
                                        —STEPHANIE ERICCSON

Which is where rituals come in.

We mark our loss symbolically—through a meaningful funeral service and burial, through days of shared grieving with family and friends, through the act of visiting the cemetery, and in other traditional rituals that have served over time.

We can also create new rituals that empower and release us from pain: a "support circle" of friends, each of whom shares his or her best memories of your mate. Lighting a candle each night for the first year of mourning. Arranging significant relics and photographs on the mantel. Writing a memoir—however informal—as a way of symbolically saying good-bye.

We sanctify this life-changing experience by naming it, honoring it, treating it with care.

AFFIRMATION: I will create meaningful rituals to mark this experience.

I am new to this thing called widowhood.
                                          —RUTH COUGHLIN

Everything about this experience is new. The pain is fresh, unlike anything we've encountered. We are novices at grieving, taking baby steps in unfamiliar terrain, unsure of ourselves, without the slightest idea of how to proceed.

Here's how: by calling upon past events of our lives that will guide us in this process: the times of sorrow we have endured; the courage we've summoned at other intersections when hope was elusive and the future unknown; the support we've given to others who stand ready with open arms; and the willingness to learn as we go, to be gentle, patient, and loving with ourselves as we begin to adjust to this unbidden, yet deeply transformative stage in our journey.

AFFIRMATION: I have my past experience to guide me.

> *I learned so many things about him from other people's memories.*
>
> —TAMAR H.

We thought we knew everything about him, then suddenly we learn something new as others share their personal memories.

We may respond in a number of ways: feeling hurt and resentful over hidden aspects of our spouse's personality we weren't aware of. Or our appreciation of him may grow through the eyes of others: His best friend relates a story about the time they went camping and our late husband talked about remnant childhood fears; co-workers regale us with anecdotes about his penchant for practical jokes, which we knew nothing about; a distant cousin takes us aside at the funeral and asks if we still have the poetry our husband wrote in his college years, and we wonder, *Why didn't he ever tell me about that?*

The answer is: All of us show different sides to different people. This is no reflection on his love or commitment, merely a tribute to how complex and multifaceted a person he was. Instead of feeling left out, we can learn more about the man we loved.

AFFIRMATION: I am still getting to know you.

So many people have offerred their condolences, sharing how highly they thought of your mate. You feel proud. You wish he could know what a lasting impact he's made.

He can. In the following space, write a letter telling him what a difference he's made and how very many people think the world of him.

My Dearest_____,

These are some of the wonderful things people have said about you: . . .

*The legacy of Arthur Ashe was not in the way he died,
but in the way he lived.*

—TELEVISION DOCUMENTARY

As time passes, we are less focused on how our spouse died
and more conscious of how he lived: what he stood for, the
work he accomplished, the causes and contributions he supported, the friendships he embraced over the course of his
life.

Tennis-great Arthur Ashe is a larger-than-life example:
We can remember his victory at Wimbledon, we can recall
the televised press conference at which he announced his
battle with AIDS. Or we can focus on how he took advantage
of his star status to educate others about this deadly disease,
at the cost of his and his family's privacy, so as to have
something positive come of his death.

Arthur Ashe's legacy is his character—how he conducted
himself on *and* off the court, in victory as well as in defeat.
So, too, with time we can refocus on the whole of our
husband's life. Rereading the eulogy and condolence notes
helps us to remember. They're a living tribute to the man
we love.

AFFIRMATION: He was a good man.

Grief can't be shared. Everyone carries it alone, his own burden, his own way.

—ANNE MORROW LINDBERGH

So many can share our sorrow in small portion. Our children's own suffering enable them to empathize; friends, in-laws, siblings, and co-workers mourn the loss of our beloved and reach out to say, "I feel for your pain."

But in truth we each grieve alone. No one can truly, fully, completely experience what it means for us to have lost the love of our life. Even another widow can only say, "This is how it was for me. How is it for you?"

How it is is lonely. And private. And incredibly, incredibly painful, one of life's heaviest burdens that each of us must get through on our own.

AFFIRMATION: I carry my burden with dignity.

> *My seminar leader said to me, "Chrissie, you should
> learn to be happy one day at a time." But you can also
> be miserable one day at a time.*
>
> —LILY TOMLIN AND JANE WAGNER

Fair enough! Slogans such as One Day at a Time imply the
possibility of finding happiness—or at least peace—in the
discipline of living for the moment, making our way through
each day as it comes. But as Lily Tomlin, in her one-woman
show, *The Search for Signs of Intelligent Life in the Universe,*
cynically reminds us, we also have to get through our misery
one day at a time. And some days misery is all we have to
show for our efforts. Some days just making it from sunup to
sundown is the best we can manage. Some days we mentally
cross off another day on the calendar, grateful that we've
survived yet one more day, hopeful that tomorrow will be
better.

Maybe, maybe not. Eventually an hour—a day, a month
—will pass in which we can genuinely say we feel more joy
than sorrow, more gratitude than despair. Meanwhile getting
through another day is a testament to our resilience, proof
positive that we can make it through another, and another,
and another.

AFFIRMATION: One day at a time.

*When you visit a mourner's house, you are not supposed
to speak until the mourner speaks to you.*

—ORTHODOX JUDAISM

In a perfect world our loved ones would take cues from us,
intuitively sensing when to speak and when to remain silent,
when to engage us in personal conversations regarding our
pain and when to wait for us to take the lead. Typically
people assume that we want and are waiting for them to ask
us how we're doing, to in some way acknowledge our grief
by expressing their condolences. We feel compelled to respond, and sometimes finding words is more of a hassle than
a comfort. We may just not feel like talking, yet we don't
want to appear ungrateful or impolite. We may also feel
defensive, as if our silence somehow reflects denial, which
certainly isn't the case.

However, since people can't be expected to read our
minds, it's up to us to let them know our needs. One widow
said she wished there was a button she could wear that read,
I Know You're Sorry, but I Just Don't Want to Talk About It
Right Now.

We can be respectful to others *and* ourselves by using
those very words:

**AFFIRMATION: I know you're sorry, but I don't want
to talk about it right now.**

What no one ever really tells you about is the one thing that should be the most obvious: that you will never see him again.

—RUTH COUGHLIN

These true, true words are from the pages of an incredibly heartbreaking memoir: *Grieving: A Love Story*. It all comes down to this: Never again will we gaze into his countenance, stroke his hair, watch him in his sleep, delight in the smile lines around his eyes. Never again will he walk through the front door, take his place at the dinner table, and regale us with stories about the details of his day. Never again will we hold his hand in a darkened movie theater, set off together on a weekend car trip, caress his shoulder as he kisses our neck.

Of course no one mentions this; imagining it is far too painful. Living it challenges us, each and every day, to say:

AFFIRMATION: I accept that I will never see him again.

Another friend had the nerve to tell me she was a "golf widow."

—ANONYMOUS WIDOW, QUOTED IN
I'm Grieving as Fast as I Can

Can you believe the things some people say?

Okay, now that we're done being outraged, let's look at this calmly. Here's what's going on: Our friends make comments like this for one reason and one reason only: It's their best shot at trying to connect, at trying to say, "See, I have problems, too, so I understand how you feel."

Of course they don't have a clue. In fact they've missed it by a mile. And of course we feel like killing them out of frustration that anyone—especially someone who cares—could be so utterly insensitive.

Comments such as these are so off the mark, they can only be combatted with a sense of humor. If anyone says anything like this, take a deep breath and say,

AFFIRMATION: "Well, you poor dear. And I thought I had problems!"

PERSPECTIVE

I think these difficult times have helped me understand better that so many things that one goes around worrying about are of no importance whatsoever.

—ISAK DINESEN

Tragedy has a way of putting everything into perspective. So much of what we used to fret, obsess, and agonize over seems trivial in light of our loss. We're clearer about what truly matters. Insignificant, situational, temporary trials have lost their power to distract and disturb us.

And that's one of the rewards of having struggled through —and survived—hard times. We reclarify our priorities, making sure they reflect our most deeply held values. Having danced with death—having suffered the deepest of all loss— we're sturdier and more able to let go of the little things, knowing that in the grand scheme they aren't worth worrying about.

AFFIRMATION: Now I know what really matters.

*It was an immense betrayal—the more terrible because
she could not grasp what had been betrayed.*

—AYN RAND

The betrayal we feel is so big, so immense, so free-floating,
at times it's difficult to pin down the exact source of our
pain. What death has taken from us is so incomprehensible,
we may not know what to focus on first. Sometimes we're
fixated on the more tangible losses: the empty house rever-
berating with silence, the bills that come in our own name,
the need to hire a snowshoveling service before the first
blizzard of the season.

Other times we're more aware of the emotional losses:
the affection we crave, the companionship we yearn for, the
spiritual emptiness we face as we grapple with the meaning
of our mate's death.

But we needn't make sense of our grief in order to express it. Insight will come slowly, in unexpected bursts of
light, as we come to grasp the full measure of our loss.

AFFIRMATION: This will all make more sense in time.

Most of us are left with some residual anger, even rage which hopefully dissipates over time. It may seem sacrilegious to rail at the dead, but it's a necessary and productive part of healing. Go ahead. In the following space write a letter to your love, telling him everything you're mad about. Begin with these words:

My Dearest_____,

   I am so angry about . . .

I equated not being miserable with not caring, and not caring was intolerable.

—XENIA ROSE

Survivor guilt affects us in two significant ways, neither of which is particularly rational. First, we hesitate to throw ourselves with gusto into enjoying our lives; how dare we laugh, lose ourselves in a movie, savor a delicious meal when he's lying cold in his grave? As Suzanne, a widow of six months says, "I felt self-conscious in front of my friends. I somehow felt as if I needed to apologize for being happy."

Second, being miserable makes us feel connected, whereas being happy feels like a betrayal of our love. It's not! It's what he'd want, and it's what you'd want for him if the situation were reversed. True love means going on with your life, hopefully with increased joy in the days to come.

AFFIRMATION: I honor his memory through happiness and joy.

The only feelings that do not change are the ones that are ignored.

—ANNE BRENER

As our days of healing go by, we may be tempted to "put away" feelings of rage, sadness, and fear—the "negative" emotions that seem destructive in nature, that keep us from functioning productively and moving on with our lives.

In fact we need to do the opposite. Not only are these feelings real, they are constructive emotions that are essential to healing. The traditional AA saying "You can't go around it, you have to go through it" applies: However painful, feelings that are ignored fester beneath the surface. If we're able to delve deeply into the source of our anguish, we emerge on the other side strengthened and ready to go on with the business of living.

Our rage, sadness, and fear *will* diminish if we make their acquaintance and let them run their course.

AFFIRMATION: I won't fool myself by ignoring the "hard feelings," hoping they'll go underground.

I play with the ring you put on my hand that glorious
day in June so many years ago.

—STEPHANIE ERICCSON

Another dilemma: What to do about our wedding ring? Do
we leave it on our finger, a symbolic commitment that carries beyond death? Do we put it away for safekeeping? Do we
wear it sometimes and not others, experimenting with what
feels right?

Some widows never remove their ring, feeling, as Ericcson writes, "I need to keep your protective circle around my
finger." Some widows hang it on a necklace close to their
heart. For others, taking it off is another step toward acknowledging and accepting the end of one stage of life and
the beginning of another.

This is a private and personal decision, which will become
clearer with time. Do whatever helps you heal.

AFFIRMATION: With this ring, I thee wed.

MONTH TWO   **DAY TWENTY-SIX**

You may forget your keys, misplace your wallet, drop a
glass, or misspell your own name—several times in a row.
—HAROLD BLOOMFIELD

"I kept joking that I had early Alzheimer's, but deep down I
was really scared I was losing it," says Jill, a forty-eight-year-
old woman whose husband died of cancer. "Fortunately,"
she says, "the other women in my support group were just
as distracted as I was. One went shopping and forgot where
she parked her car. She was in a total panic until the security
guard at the mall drove her around until they found it."

We may laugh about it later, but in the first weeks of
mourning it's plenty frightening to find ourselves this out of
touch. Until it passes, here are a few memory aides to reduce anxiety: (a) Always put your keys, wallet, and valuables
in the same place; (b) make lists (grocery lists, to-do lists,
phone-number lists) instead of relying on memory.

Above all else, *slow down*! Moderating your pace, focusing
on only one thing at a time, is the best way of keeping your
head straight enough to handle everything facing you right
now.

AFFIRMATION: I'll readjust my expectations.

A widow, it seems, becomes an instant threat to wives.
—DR. JOYCE BROTHERS

This is one of the most disturbingly common experiences widows report: longtime women friends who suddenly pull away for fear of a "single woman" threatening their marriage.

It's a shame. This is one time when we need our friends' support. If ever women ought to come through for one another, it's during life-cycle losses, when we truly need comfort and companionship.

Feeling threatened, however, *is* understandable on two counts: Insecure friends may worry that a widow's perceived availability may be seductive to their spouse. The proximity of a widow also evokes fear of their own mortality; if this could happen to her, it could happen to me!

None of which excuses the behavior. If this happens to you, it's best to let go of the friendship, instead spending time with people who can only give you unconditional love and support.

AFFIRMATION: I won't squander time and energy on bitterness.

> *There is a Jewish mourning custom of covering the mirrors in the house.*
>
> —ANNE BRENER

This custom goes on from the moment of death until the end of shiva, the seven-day period following the burial. This author offers the following explanation for this custom: "Vanity has no place in a house of mourning. After a death, we need to dwell on issues of the soul, not on eternal concerns that are reinforced by viewing one's own reflection."

In other words covering the mirrors keeps us from focusing on superficial concerns with our appearance, instead training our gaze inward, where the true spiritual meaning of our experience is revealed.

Covering mirrors is of course both a concrete exercise and a meaningful metaphor; we can reach the same ends through various means—by wearing simple, unadorned attire; by not indulging in socializing, drinking, shopping, or other recreational activities; by putting mundane tasks aside, spending our time in prayer and meditation.

What matters is to turn away from our mirrors, our distractions, our ordinary concerns so as to be fully engaged in our bereavement.

AFFIRMATION: I won't distract myself from my grief.

I woke up this morning without you. Don't ask me how but I got through.

—IRIS DEMENT

Waking up in the morning without him is the first—and in some ways, the hardest—challenge we face. Each sunrise reminds us of his absence; each morning at breakfast we sit alone, once again having to overcome the hurdle of getting through yet another day without our beloved.

And each day we somehow manage to meet the challenge. We get up, we get dressed, we check our to-do list and resolve to rise to the occasion as best we can. There is no way to avoid the pain of remembering, no way to get around the sick feeling in the pit of our stomach, the ache in our heart as morning comes and we face the stark, irrefutable fact of our loss. At first, when we get to the end of the day, we say to ourselves, *Don't ask me how, but I got through.* As time passes, we are surprised by how much easier it's become. We may even find ourselves saying, *Not only did I get through, I even had a pretty good day.*

Then the sun rises on a new day—and again we wake up without him, and it still hurts, and it will for a while.

AFFIRMATION: I've made it through another day.

> *Of late she had learned that happy people hate the unhappy.*
>
> —REBECCA WEST

We may find ourselves in the awkward position of sensing—even blatantly experiencing—other people's retreat from our company. There's no way around it—with the exception of close friends and relatives, other people have a limited tolerance (and often a distaste) for our pain and unhappiness.

There are many understandable reasons why friends may keep their distance: They feel helpless and therefore uncomfortable when dealing with us. Our loss threatens their sense of security. It simply bums them out; their happiness is contingent on avoiding exposure to pain.

There's not a whole lot we can do about this, other than to carefully choose involvements with people who have the capacity to accept us as we are and to call upon their own store of energy to give us love and support.

AFFIRMATION: I will spend my time with friends who are strong enough to support my grieving.

I was convinced that I was being ignored and forgotten.
—PHILOMENE GATES

It's natural to feel ignored and forgotten, especially in the first few weeks following the funeral. The phone stops ringing, the plants and fruit baskets stop being delivered, the flood of well-wishers begins to wane, and we begin to wonder if their condolences were sincere.

They were. But at some point even the closest friends and relatives must return to their lives. Meanwhile you get to feel sorry for yourself. For a while, that is. How long is a while? Until your hurt and self-righteousness result in pushing away the love you need.

When self-pity turns self-destructive, it's time to do something positive to turn the situation around. If you feel ignored and forgotten, get on the phone and start making plans. Take the first step and it's likely to be reciprocated.

AFFIRMATION: I will make the first move.

Are Your Support Systems in Place?

Some of us are fortunate to have a reliable circle of supportive family and friends. Some of us have to make an extra effort now that we're alone. But even if we're surrounded by love, we may find it healing to seek out other widows with whom we can share the uniqueness of this experience. Because no matter how hard anyone tries to identify with what we're feeling, there's no better support than someone who has been there, who is traveling the same rocky terrain.

Churches, synagogues, therapists, and community agencies are good places to seek support. A "buddy system" will serve you well, especially in those moments when it seems like no one else can possibly understand.

I stare at Mel's picture. Suddenly my hand moves in a swift gesture, as though slapping him across the face. "Why did you leave me?" I scream at him.

—ANNE HOSANSKY

Rage. Blind fury at the horrible injustice of having lost the one we so dearly loved.

It's a powerful emotion. And it's an appropriate response to the wounds sustained. We may find ourselves lashing out at others or at God, screaming and wailing, erupting with rage so fierce, it scares us to realize how angry we are.

We should be. What's happened isn't fair; expressing anger is part of the grieving process. So let it all out. Without being abusive, perhaps with the help of a counselor, go ahead and pound your pillow, release your rage, over and over, until it naturally, gradually lessens and fades.

AFFIRMATION: I have every right to my anger.

No one will ever love me the way he did.
                                                —MANY WIDOWS

It's true. No matter how many friends we have, no matter who we meet in the future, no one will ever love us quite as much as our mate. The special way he stroked our hair, his stupid jokes that made us laugh, his unique ability to comfort and reassure us can never, ever be replaced.

Knowing this can make us feel lost and despondent. I felt this way after my divorce; I was convinced that I'd never meet anyone, ever again, who would love and care for me like my husband.

And I didn't. But since then I've met others who, each in their own way, have brought me happiness and joy. We needn't reject overtures in order to honor our beloved, nor does loving again in any way diminish our devotion to the deceased. We open ourselves to new relationships with these words:

AFFIRMATION: I can love and be loved again.

> *But then I remember I am making this "killing" only because Len is dead. And suddenly I feel a whiplash of guilt.*
>
> —REBECCA RICE

This goes in the category entitled Needless Guilt. You're not alone in feeling it, but it serves absolutely no purpose other than to exacerbate your pain.

Because the fact is if you inherited money, then it's yours, and you may as well enjoy it. Even if (God forbid!) you were desperately short of cash and had fantasized relief upon your spouse's deathbed, that doesn't make you a gravedigger, by any stretch of the imagination. For one thing, as his wife you are entitled to whatever monetary settlement has resulted from his death. More importantly he'd want you to be as comfortable and secure as possible under the circumstances.

So relax. Accept the money graciously, and if there's any extra, make a contribution in his memory.

AFFIRMATION: I am entitled to feel secure.

DETACHMENT

I feel withdrawn, aloof, almost watching my own life from above.

—JONATHAN LAZEAR

In the earliest stage of grief our denial creates a trancelike state in which we go through the motions of our daily life without feeling much of anything.

One widow describes this phenomenon as "watching myself almost as if I was in a movie. During the last few days at the hospice, through the funeral, and for several weeks afterward," she says, "I merely went through the motions like a robot programmed to cope."

Detachment is a necessary defense mechanism until we are ready to feel the full extent of our anger, bargaining, depression, and finally the acceptance that comes later in the grieving process. Feeling numb doesn't mean avoidance, it's just a helpful gift to get you through this time.

AFFIRMATION: My distance is a natural response to emotional overload.

Had Julie not been the deceased, it was a funeral she would have loved.

—ERMA BOMBECK

Our mate's funeral is the first of so many emotional events we will experience without him. In a strange and ironic way we wish he could have been there—to hear the loving way in which he was eulogized, to see how many people cared enough to pay their respects. Perhaps he would have been moved by our choice of music, the sonnet we read, the somber processional of pallbearers, including his brothers, sons, and closest of friends. He probably would have chuckled at the funny anecdote the minister shared; he certainly would have wiped away the tears streaming down our face.

Arranging and carrying out our spouse's funeral was a final act of devotion. Amid our pain we can take pleasure in knowing we did it right, that we made him proud, that we publicly honored him in a way he would have loved and appreciated.

AFFIRMATION: The funeral was just right.

It seems strange that he missed the funeral; it may be your first significant experience without him.

But we can give him the details. In the following space write a letter, telling your departed spouse all about the funeral—the music, the eulogy, who attended, and most importantly how you felt. Begin with these words:

My Dearest_____,

   The funeral was . . .

I poured the ashes out into a bowl and looked at them.
Dug my hand into what was left of you.

—ANN, *Exposure*

If our mate was cremated, we are left with his ashes; Emily
refers to her late husband, Charlie's, urn as "the essence of
my beloved."

Widows react in various ways to their beloved's remains;
some are comforted by the sight of the urn, some are re-
pulsed, but all are faced with figuring out whether to keep
them and where (on the mantel? on the nightstand?),
whether to dispose of them and where, and when is the right
time to do anything at all.

My dear friends Jeff and Jan waited four months before
wading into the headwaters of the Mississippi with their still-
born son, Logan's, ashes, tearfully releasing them into the
river's flow.

Finding the right way to handle our mate's ashes is one of
the hardest, most powerfully healing aspects of mourning.
Wait until you know what's best for you, what will honor
him and bring you peace.

AFFIRMATION: Ashes to ashes, dust to dust.

*I spent hours worrying about money, sure I would end
up as a bag lady.*

—DR. JOYCE BROTHERS

This, from a woman with a thriving, lucrative career (not to
mention marriage to a successful surgeon), reveals how universally widows worry about money, regardless of economic
status.

For some, being widowed *does* have serious financial
repercussions; we may find ourselves having to sell our
home, find a job, or dramatically downsize in order to keep
our heads above water. Even women with a fair share of
economic security worry about ending up destitute, of being
out in the street, destined to be "bag ladies" without their
husband's support. We go over the checkbook repeatedly,
making budgets and obsessing over even the smallest expenditures until we're sure that we can make it on our own.

This situation calls for action: whether or not you *actually*
have enough, if you're worrying about money, do whatever
it takes to ease your fears by finding a trusted financial adviser, putting your books in order, and making any lifestyle
changes that will help ease your mind.

**AFFIRMATION: This is another way I am putting my
life in order.**

Have You Renegotiated Membership Dues,
Charitable Contributions,
and Other Monetary Expenses
According to
Your Present Economic Status?

This can go either way. The financial situation of some widows is improved, others have to tighten their belt. If you fall into the former category, consider your increased contribution as another way of honoring your spouse. If you fall into the latter category, there's nothing to be ashamed of. Whether it's a matter of increasing your pledge or cutting back, renegotiating fiscal commitments is another necessary piece of business to tackle. The majority of widows experience the need to cut expenses; you shouldn't be expected to keep up with promises made prior to your mate's death.

Taking care of this task may be easiest to do in writing. Or with the help of a financial adviser or friend.

SUSTENANCE

Enough with the feelings. Bring me some matzoh-ball soup.

—SUSAN JACOBY

As Susan Jacoby pointed out in *The New York Times,* words only go so far in their capacity to comfort us. After a while all the *I'm sorry*s and *I wish I could do something*s get stale: we wish that others would express their care in more tangible ways—bringing chicken soup, running errands, making concrete contributions to lighten our load.

It's so hard to tell our loved ones what's helpful and what's not. We feel pushy, ungrateful, and uncomfortable spelling out our needs. But no one can be expected to read our minds. If it's soup you crave, say so. If it's help writing thank-you notes, let a friend know. Remember, friends and relatives *want* to help. Help *them* by being specific about what would make a difference.

AFFIRMATION: I need . . .

*My heating pad was a comforting source of warmth when
I started to sleep alone.*

—LYNN CAINE

Teddy bears, extra pillows and blankets, even sleeping pads
are all ways of generating warmth and finding something to
hold on to instead of him.

Some widows have gone to great length to find a substitute; one woman bought a life-size doll, which she placed in
bed next to her the whole first year after her husband died.
Another filled her bed with stuffed animals; still another
invited her two cats into her bed.

There's no shame in needing comfort. After years of
snuggling, the bed can feel cold and lonely; do whatever
helps you curl up and get some sleep.

AFFIRMATION: I will keep myself safe and warm.

Have You Bought Yourself New Sheets?

Buying brand-new sheets—and maybe even pillows and comforters—requires that you take a number of difficult and important steps forward: (a) It involves shopping, which in itself is an affirmative act; (b) it's a lovely gift to ourselves, which is surprisingly difficult to indulge in and which is a concrete way of valuing ourselves; (c) it symbolizes acknowledging our willingness not only to sleep alone but to take pleasure in crisp, virginal new sheets, untouched by any human body other than our own.

I did it after my divorce. Lots of widows have made it a ritual act of accepting their single status. We feel both sorrow and excitement in symbolically making our own, new bed.

The word courage *derives from* coeur, *the French word for "heart."*

—JOHN WELWOOD

The writer goes on to say that the essence of courage is being willing to feel our heart even in situations that are difficult or painful.

I like this definition; it implies a softening of our heart rather than a hardening of will in order to survive.

Many people think that courage is a matter of squaring our shoulders and pushing through our pain. In truth vulnerability is the prerequisite to courage. Bravery in the face of loss is measured by our willingness to transcend bravado for the far more difficult task of allowing our sadness to surface, our anguish to be exposed.

We pray for the courage to let our hearts lead the way, to feel the full measure of our loss.

AFFIRMATION: I am brave enough to let my heart crack open.

*A wild protest stormed up in him against the horror of
it, its senseless waste of life, its wanton cruelty.*
—MILTON STEINBERG

Grieving is often described as emotional protest: we cry out
against the horror, the injustice, the senseless cruelty of what
has been taken from us.

In the most intense moments of mourning we may find
ourselves saying over and over, "NO! This just cannot be!"
This is different from denial; protest is a militant stand
against injustice, the bridge between denial and anger, between numbness and full-blown rage at what is implicitly
unfair, at what is undeniably unacceptable.

Protesting the injustice of our mate's death is empowering
if taken to the next step, which is action. We combat injustice through acts of healing: giving meaning to our loss by
creating a memorial fund in our spouse's name, fund-raising
for the particular illness that he died of, volunteering at a
hospice, or any other way in which we positively channel our
rage.

AFFIRMATION: I rage at the injustice of your death.

I've fallen into a common trap of widowhood. It's called Sanctifying the Spouse. Saint Mel wouldn't recognize himself.

—ANNE HOSANSKY

At first we only remember the wonderful things about our mate, blanking out the frustrations and difficulties we struggled with when he was alive. We want to hold on to a "perfect picture," yet, as most widows realize, it's a trap. Pretending he was a saint doesn't serve us *or* him. Remembering him as a whole person, complete with both strengths and limitations, allows us to have *all* of our feelings, the good ones as well as the ones that weren't so good. We can only forgive him for the tough times if we're willing to recall him honestly for he who was. Likewise it doesn't serve him to enshrine his memory. There's nothing noble about reinventing him postmortem. The person you loved was a real, perfectly flawed human—nothing more, nothing less.

AFFIRMATION: I will remember him as he was.

There's an abyss between us. I feel as if I'm exiled in an alien country they [friends] know nothing about.
— Xenia Rose

And of course, they can't. Regardless of how loving and well-intentioned friends try to be, there is no possible way for anyone to understand fully what we are going through. We have traveled emotional terrain they have blessedly been spared; even those who have experienced similar losses fall short of being able fully to appreciate the depth of our pain.

Which leaves us two choices: We can isolate ourselves by focusing on the differences, the ways in which our pain is utterly unique and unfathomable. Or we can find the common ground, bridging the abyss through the empathy born of similar life experiences.

We can also take the opportunity to teach. We have learned so much in our journey. Now we can help others prepare for what inevitably lies ahead.

AFFIRMATION: I will reach across the gulf.

Then there's remorse: If only I'd taken better care of him . . . if I had insisted he slow down, or had eaten more sensibly, or not driven so fast.

—PHILOMENE GATES

GIVE IT UP!

Beating ourselves up for ways in which we imagine we might have prevented his death is arrogant *and* an awful waste of energy.

The truth is no matter how much we loved him, no matter how diligently we cared for him, we're not God. We aren't responsible for our spouse's death, and there's nothing we could have done about it. Remorse won't bring him back; thinking otherwise is simply a distraction—a way of focusing on *what if*s instead of what is.

Some events are strictly beyond our control. Accepting that his death was inevitable—destined, if you will—is yet another way in which we let go of the past so that we can live fully, freely in the present.

AFFIRMATION: I couldn't have saved him.

If we're riddled (or even somewhat troubled) with feelings of guilt, it's time to unburden ourselves. In the following space take the opportunity to tell your husband anything and everything you feel remorseful about. Your feelings needn't be rational; just be honest, perhaps by using these words:

My Dearest_____,

   I feel so guilty about . . .

MONTH THREE   **DAY TWENTY-ONE**

The most striking Jewish expression of grief is the rending of garments by the mourner prior to the funeral service.

—MAURICE LAMM

In Jewish tradition, right before the funeral a black ribbon is pinned on the immediate family members' clothing, then ripped, to symbolize the tear in their hearts. Then a black ribbon, worn throughout the entire first year of mourning, is pinned to their garment.

This ritual is a powerful metaphor for loss, reminding us of our tangible loss, separating us from others and signaling our formal state of bereavement.

In many cultures throughout the world black is worn by widows and others who are in mourning. While wearing dark clothing can be a daily expression of our somber mood, some find it intensifies depression. Like so many aspects of healing, this is a personal choice. Do it if it helps you heal. Don't feel pressured if it increases your pain and discomfort.

AFFIRMATION: I will find the right personal expression for my mourning.

For the first time in thirty-nine years, they have different addresses. His is: Riverside Cemetery, Plot 12, Row E.
—ANNE HOSANSKY

Harsh words—poignant, tragic, and just about as real as it gets.

There is such finality to saying these words out loud: "My husband and I no longer live under the same roof." "The love of my life is buried six feet under the ground." "I am alive. He is dead."

Facing reality is an essential part of grieving. Only when we truly accept that he's never coming home, that we are truly on our own, can we move on to rebuild our lives in the present.

Regular visits to the cemetery are an important part of rebuilding and reconciling ourselves to reality. Each time we place flowers on his grave, offering words of prayer and gratitude, we say good-bye again; each time with greater confidence we say, despite the pain, that we are on the road to recovery.

AFFIRMATION: We may live apart, but you will always have a place in my heart.

The raw gaping hole in the earth, open to receive the coffin, symbolizes the raw emptiness of the mourner.
—AUDREY GORDON

The Jewish tradition of mourning includes a ritual of shoveling dirt onto the casket as it's lowered into the grave. Immediate family members and close friends each take a turn at this hands-on participation in the burial process.

The first time I witnessed this ritual, I was appalled. It seemed unnecessarily morbid; it appeared that the bereaved were actually throwing shovelfuls of dirt onto their beloved, facilitating his or her descent into the ground.

In fact that's exactly the point. In recent years, as I've shared in this ritual, I've come to understand its significance. Rather than just being spectators, we, the bereaved, play an active role in paying our respect by helping to bury our loved ones.

AFFIRMATION: I have helped lay you to rest.

SPIRITUAL DETACHMENT

> *Everything must be parted from what it desires in the end.*
>
> —BUDDHIST BELIEF

Buddhism is filled with wisdom that's absolutely right on, yet terribly difficult to achieve.

The concept of spiritual detachment is perhaps the best example of this. It is simply true that everything we love and treasure is impermanent, that ultimately we will need to part ways. Whether it's material belongings or our beloved, we are destined to let go of all that we hold dear.

Which is of course a challenging paradox. On the one hand loving our departed mate required our willingness to give our all, to give ourselves over in every conceivable way. Yet even as we attach ourselves, we are required to divest, to understand that true love asks that we graciously part ways.

AFFIRMATION: Parting is such sweet sorrow.

A life I didn't choose
chose me: even
my tools are the wrong ones
for what I have to do.

—ADRIENNE RICH

There's a saying going around, often used when we resent the hand we've been dealt: "I didn't sign up for this," we say, and we mean, "How come this is happening to me? I'm not the least bit interested in this particular challenge."

Of course no one asked us whether we were "up" for the challenges of widowhood, and most of us don't feel we're prepared. How could we be? Until we're in the throes of it, there's no real way to sharpen our grieving skills, to practice being alone, to hone the art of grieving, to find the tools necessary to carve out a new life.

Consequently we find ourselves in an accelerated learning curve. We learn as we go, choosing to do our best at the life that's chosen us.

AFFIRMATION: I accept the challenges I've been given.

Often the test of courage is not to die, but to live.
—ANONYMOUS

In my estimation the test of courage *always* is to live, to get up in the morning, no matter how blue we feel, and do what it takes to get through the day.

And there are days—especially in the first few months of bereavement—when "living" is reduced to the basics, when going through the motions is as good as it gets. It's our best shot, and it's sufficient.

Later in our healing our definition of living expands to include work, friendships, and the creative pursuits that add quality to our days.

For a while we may question whether any of it's worth it. We ask, "What's the point of living if I can't have my mate at my side?" We may even say, "I may as well be dead." It takes courage to live despite our despair. We reward ourselves with these words:

AFFIRMATION: I courageously choose life.

If we are coping magnificently, shedding no tears and carrying on as if nothing has happened, we are only deceiving ourselves.

—JUDITH VIORST

Coping—carrying on as if it's business as usual—has been drummed into us. We may feel pressured to hold ourselves together for others' sake so as to relieve their sadness, discomfort, and helplessness. Or we may put ourselves on autopilot as protection against experiencing the full brunt of our sorrow, which if unleashed seems like an infinite, uncontrollable torrent that will sweep us under, rendering us incapable of getting through the day.

But putting up a good front simply complicates the healing process; acting as if everything's okay prevents us from venting our sorrow and getting the support we need.

We must give ourselves permission to remove our facade, let down and let go of our need to stay "strong." Real strength returns when we allow ourselves to grieve.

AFFIRMATION: It's okay to act as if everything isn't okay.

Don't trust nothin' except your instinct.

—FORREST GUMP

Sage advice. And right now advice seems to be what we're given, often unsolicited from well-meaning friends who are sure they know what we need.

But what we need is to listen to ourselves, to trust our instinct even when it flies in the face of conventional wisdom.

"Just about everyone I knew said it was a terrible idea for me to move in with my daughter and son-in-law, but it's turned out great," says one widow, Pamela, who went against advice from her friends and her therapist, doing what *she* knew was right. Carla started dating just six weeks after her husband, Randy, died, refusing to be swayed by others' blatant disapproval. Still another widow, Suzanne, chose not to attend a grief support group even though it was highly recommended by her minister, because as she says, "It may be good for others, but I'd be uncomfortable, and that's all that counts!"

Trusting our instinct may be especially difficult right now; crisis tends to lessen our confidence. If anything, we're less sure of ourselves, more likely to follow other people's direction. But if ever we needed to learn how to listen to ourselves, it's now!

AFFIRMATION: I can't go wrong if I trust my gut.

Some people think doctors and nurses can put scrambled eggs back in the shell.

—DOROTHY CANFIELD FISHER

We may feel cynical and angry at the doctor's inability to reduce our mate's pain, to sidestep seemingly unnecessary and invasive procedures, to prolong our beloved's life instead of standing helplessly by.

They call it practicing medicine and here's what it means: Medical professionals aren't miracle workers, they're simply doing their best at what is still an imperfect science. Having grown up with the belief that doctors were gods, or as close as it gets, it's natural to resent their fallibility, to direct our rage at the healer instead of at the sickness that robbed us of so much.

It may help to make an appointment with the purpose of talking through your husband's medical history, so that you can quiet any doubts you might have as to choices that were made in the course of treatment. But be careful not to be abusive. Remember, doctors are human; they, too, have feelings.

AFFIRMATION: I forgive my husband's medical providers for being fallible human beings.

Have You Resolved Any Lingering Questions About Your Husband's Medical Care?

Widows often remain confused and/or angry at the medical care their beloved received. We may not have understood complicated procedures or medical jargon; we may feel justifiably (or unreasonably) enraged that in the final analysis our spouse died despite his doctor's care.

Call, write, or make an appointment if you need more information. Don't put this off; you deserve answers to your questions.

I tasted thee, and now hunger and thirst for thee.
—SAINT AUGUSTINE

We feel a constant ache within. Having drunk from the seemingly eternal spring of his love, we wander, parched in the desert, wondering if our thirst will ever be quenched. Having dined at the banquet table, rapturously satiated, we hunger for the most paltry of crumbs, starved for his sustenance.

Had we never tasted love, our loss wouldn't be nearly so palpable. And we would never have felt so full. We may always crave his touch, his smell, the sweet taste of his love, but with time our thirst and hunger will subside.

AFFIRMATION: I remember how sweet you tasted.

MONTH FOUR   **DAY TWO**

> *And it is still true, no matter how old you are—when*
> *you go out into the world, it is best to hold hands.*
> —ROBERT FULGHUM

Holding hands is one of the things we miss most; sauntering down the street, hands clasped; clutching his hand in a darkened movie theater; feeling the comfort of his larger hand enclosing ours when we feel frightened or anxious, reassuring us we weren't alone in the world.

And we still need someone's hand to hold on to. We're used to the "buddy system," to the safety and security of being part of a pair. Some of us are fortunate to have children or friends whose hands we can freely hold: I will always be grateful to my friend, Jill, who at odd moments following my divorce—sitting in the synagogue at Friday-night services or at a party where my ex-husband appeared—spontaneously, intuitively reached out her hand.

"I spend lots of time holding my grandchildren's hands," says Liz, and it's one of the best antidotes of all. The next time you miss his hand, visit your favorite child and say:

AFFIRMATION: Here, take my hand.

I don't agree with New Age people who say things always work out. Things don't always work out.

—SUSAN GRIFFIN

Our New Age, self-help culture has created the widely held beliefs that "everything happens for a good reason" and that "things always work out for the best."

These slogans may seem facile—or downright offensive—rationalizations for what in our mind is wholly unjustifiable. In other words, we don't want to hear such esoteric explanations, mostly because they're just not true. Furthermore, they don't make a dent in our pain, because there *isn't* a good reason for our beloved's death; there's little, if any, redeeming value; and nothing has worked out the way we'd hoped.

Ultimately we come to a place of peace, not by putting a positive twist on our loss but by feeling the full fury of our pain.

AFFIRMATION: I still haven't come up with a "good reason" for my mate's death—and that's okay.

Hope is the feeling that the feeling you have isn't permanent.

—JEAN KERR

If I were to choose one quote to be copied and put on our refrigerators, this would win hands down.

Why? For three reasons: (a) It suggests that hope is the ultimate goal of grief and healing, which I soundly support; (b) it affirms that our feelings of hopelessness are real and appropriate responses to our loss; and (c) above all else it reminds us that our sorrow is temporary, a positive promise to hold on to in our darkest moments, when we fear that pain is our permanent destiny.

So many widows agree. Time and time again I've heard this comment: "The one thing that kept me going was remembering that I wouldn't always feel this way." Some people say, "I can endure anything as long as I know it will eventually end."

Our feelings will ebb and flow, changing subtly all the time. Tomorrow will be better than today—and the next day and the next. Patiently we await the return of happiness.

AFFIRMATION: I know I won't always feel this way.

- *Sundays are the worst.*
- *Holidays are the second worst.*
- *Saturday nights aren't much fun either.*

—HAROLD BLOOMFIELD

It's a toss-up. Depending on the past rhythm of our married life, weekends may be toughest, especially since they come like clockwork, each time presenting us with the challenge of filling our time and coping with our loneliness. Saturday night—"date night"—can be brutal, particularly in the area of romance and lovemaking. Sunday mornings, on the other hand—lying in bed with the newspaper, sipping coffee, working in the garden—may seem painfully empty without our buddy and companion.

And then there are holidays—emotional minefields— those ritual family events that have suddenly gone from joyous celebrations to painful reminders of our loss.

There's no way to get around the pain. There are, however, ways to lessen it: by making definite plans so that we don't find ourselves alone on Christmas or Passover. By making a point of doing something especially nice for ourselves—a New Year's makeover, a poinsettia, or a gallon of eggnog to enhance the festivities. But mostly the only antidote to "holiday blues" is time. It gets easier, but it's never quite the same.

AFFIRMATION: I'll face each challenge as it comes.

Have You Made Definite Plans for the Holidays?

Advance preparation for Christmas, New Year's, Passover, and other traditional holidays will make these occasions less painful and more palpable.

Particularly during the first few years following your spouse's death, these holidays can be excruciatingly lonely reminders of loss. In the following space write down your plans for holidays in the upcoming year. If you haven't made them, now's the time to get started.

AFFIRMATION: Here are my plans:
  • I will spend Christmas or Hanukkah with . . .
  • I will celebrate Passover or Easter by . . .
  • I will have my Thanksgiving dinner with . . .
  • I will celebrate my birthday by . . .

Friends and relatives start treating you like a child.
—LOTS OF WIDOWS

Why is it that friends and relatives tend to infantilize us, as if our grief and our new status as widows reduce and diminish us so that we're no longer capable of caring for ourselves?

This is due partly to sympathy and partly to sexism. When our loved ones feel powerless to ease our pain, they may start to coddle us as a way of showing love. It's the only way they know; treating us as if we're helpless lessens their feelings of impotence.

More insidiously, our culture tends to treat widows as if we've regressed, as if our status renders us incompetent, as if our husband handled everything, so that naturally we now need someone else to take over.

But we don't. We are full-grown adults, fully capable of handling anything and everything that comes our way. If we need help, we'll ask, thank you very much.

AFFIRMATION: I am a mature woman, capable of caring for myself.

CURIOSITY

Curiosity can be a valuable instrument or a nuisance.
—ANONYMOUS

"If one more person asks me exactly how Nate died, I think I'll scream!" says Laura, who spent nearly a year at her husband's hospice bedside as he waged a losing battle against liver cancer.

Some questions are welcome—genuine inquiries from friends whose intentions are to comprehend the full measure of our loss. Others are intrusive—just old-fashioned bad taste—curiosity seekers asking for details that are none of their business and only make us feel worse.

Under *no* circumstances are you obligated to respond. You can walk away *or,* if you wish, answer by saying:

AFFIRMATION: I'd rather not go into it.

Death is not the end; there remains the litigation.
—AMBROSE BIERCE

It's heartbreaking when family members contest the will, fight over inheritances, or engage in any other legal conflict that creates bitterness on top of grief.

This scenario occurs regularly in blended families. As Randi, who was widowed after her second husband died, recalls, "As if I wasn't in enough pain, I had to sit through a horrible court hearing during which Frank's two grown children tried to convince the judge that I had no right to the money I'd been bequeathed. They even said, 'Our father only married her because he was lonely,' which had me in tears, even though I knew it wasn't true."

If you find yourself in this unfortunate situation, here's my advice: Take the high ground. Fight for what's yours, but be sure to conduct yourself graciously, without rancor or ugly confrontations. If it helps, remember, those who are opposing you are acting out of their pain.

AFFIRMATION: I won't lower myself to their level.

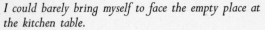

I could barely bring myself to face the empty place at the kitchen table.

—NAN S.

It's the "widow diet," and while it may be grand to drop a few pounds, ultimately not eating is a dangerous side effect of grief. We need our energy, we need to remain healthy. Stopping eating is a sure way of lowering our immunity and putting ourselves at risk.

For many of us dinner was the primary meal at which we connected with our spouse. Now it's another hurdle. The "empty place" may as well be a flashing billboard: He's Gone. You're Alone. Now See How Great the Meat Loaf Tastes! It probably tastes like cardboard, or worse, which is why it's important to find ways to be nourished without feeling devastated.

Here are a few suggestions from experts:

- Eat small meals. High-protein snacks can replace sit-down dinners for now.
- Eat in front of the television or while reading a book—anything to distract you.
- Invite a friend to dinner at least once a week.
- Change where you eat. Instead of the dining room, curl up on the couch or bed with a tray.
- Take supplements. Vitamins and other nutritional supplements will help compensate until your appetite returns.

AFFIRMATION: I will do my best to eat.

Are You Eating Nutritiously?

Back to the basics. A healthy diet is often one of the first things to go when we're grieving. Consequently we must take special care to make sure we're eating nutritious meals and taking supplements if necessary.

Even if you have to force yourself, don't neglect yourself in this very important way. Make this commitment to your own health; nourishment helps us heal.

Grief is a physical pain. In the breast. I didn't know that before.

—JILL TRUMAN

We say, "My heart is aching"—describing the intensely physical pain that accompanies our grief.

Our anguish is manifested throughout our being: We are bone-weary with overwhelming fatigue; we have a flulike malaise from our fingers to our toes. "I felt as if I'd been run over by a truck," says Lynn, describing the profound physical pain she experienced during the first three months after her husband died.

Just as the sorrow lessens, our aches and pains diminish with time. But for now we need to be gentle with ourselves. Sleep helps. Fresh air, exercise, good food, and massage are great antidotes. There's nothing self-indulgent about pampering ourselves right now; it's essential to recovery and healing.

Especially if widowhood followed months of caring for our late spouse, we need now to lavish attention on ourselves.

AFFIRMATION: It's my turn to be pampered.

Have You Had a Complete Medical Checkup?

Research has revealed that grief lowers our immunity, increasing our susceptibility to illness. For this reason it's important to pay attention to your health by having a full medical checkup as part of your healing process.

This is another way of taking care of ourselves and assuming responsibility for our lives.

Twenty-eight years is a long time that vanishes in the instant of a diagnosis.

—JOAN GOULD

With the exception of women for whom widowhood happened in an unexpected tragedy, the moment we heard the worst remains forever embedded in memory. "I'm sorry, it's terminal. There's nothing we can do." Time stopped, and in an instant our lives were irrevocably altered. Sitting in the doctor's office, taking in the weight of words so incomprehensible, we were sure we must be in the midst of a nightmare, from which we would surely awake. And so we began the long journey from denial to acceptance. In the process, time itself was experienced in a whole new way. Every moment was precious, every encounter enhanced by wondering if it may be the last. Hopefully we used the time well—expressing all the things we had to say, making amends, saying good-bye in so many different ways in the remaining hours and days.

AFFIRMATION: I commit myself to making the most of each day.

There is nothing more demoralizing than sudden, overwhelming disillusionment.

—DOROTHY THOMPSON

We feel cheated. Cynical. Unwilling to put our faith in much of anything, when so much we believed in—and so much we held dear—has been taken away.

Disillusionment is another necessary step in the grieving process. It involves stripping away our illusions—that our marriage was forever, that we would never be alone, that the combination of our love and modern medicine could work miracles—leaving us with the harsh reality we are forced to reckon with.

Yet reality is the pathway to sanity. The truth is nothing is forever. Ultimately each of us is alone. All the love, medicine, and miracles couldn't save him, despite everyone's best efforts.

And so there is nothing left but acceptance. As we make peace with reality, we free ourselves to heal and once again find hope.

AFFIRMATION: I am grappling with reality.

You might as well live.

—DOROTHY PARKER

It is the rare widow who doesn't contemplate whether or not it's worth it to go on living. Even when we rationally know better, there are times when it seems worthless to go on. Our anguish makes us question the value of existence; our depression makes us hard-pressed to find the inspiration and motivation to embrace the future without our beloved traveling companion.

But as Dorothy Parker dryly put it, you might as well live. After all, what's the alternative? We can give in to despair *or* we can slowly, but surely, pick up the pieces. Doing so requires a leap of faith: that our energy and vitality will return; that we will find new meaning in the ongoing pursuit of work, friendships, and other involvements; that the future will hold a measure of peace and happiness if we allow ourselves to be open to the possibility and are willing to say:

AFFIRMATION: I still have so much to live for.

The dead don't have to clean up their own messes. They don't have to straighten out the late bills, the lost wills, the floundering business investments.

—STEPHANIE ERICCSON

This is the truest meaning of the term *unfinished business,* and it is one of the most frustrating aspects of death that most, if not all, of us deal with. It's the rare person whose affairs are completely in order. Depending on circumstances, we may have numerous "messes" to clean up, and we are understandably angered. Not only are we emotionally abandoned, now we are left with bills to pay, calls to make, perhaps even conflicts that need patching up in order to reconcile relationships in the wake of his death.

It's okay to be mad. It's not fair; it's simply the price we pay for years of partnership. Remember "for better or for worse"—and this is "for worse." It's necessary, and the sooner we handle it, the better we'll feel.

AFFIRMATION: I'll take care of this too.

No matter how many conversations we had prior to his death, there may be still details we need information about: where he put the wrench, where he put the life-insurance forms, the exact price he negotiated with the painter that day he came to give an estimate for the house.

The following exercise is not going to yield answers. What it *will* do is clarify projects that need attention and motivate you to do what it takes.

My Dearest_____,

Could you please tell me where . . .

There is no such thing as security. There never has been.
—GERMAINE GREER

The loss of security is one of the casualties of widowhood. We thought we were safe and secure, that we could count on our mate's emotional, physical, and financial support.

But permanent security is an illusion. Sooner or later we realize that each of us is a separate individual, solely responsible for our own well-being. And so we have one more thing to grieve. We have learned an important lesson: that no matter how much we love and are committed to another human being, ultimately we are on our own. Knowing this empowers us to cultivate self-reliance, freeing us to love again someday, with the understanding that:

AFFIRMATION: The only security is knowing I can take care of myself.

LAUGHTER

That is the best—to laugh with someone because you both think the same things are funny.
—GLORIA VANDERBILT

Mutual laughter is magical; for many of us it is one of the most sorely missed and most irreplaceable aspects of losing our loved one. The private jokes and shared sensibilities spoke volumes of how very much we trusted and understood one another. Over years we communicated in shorthand—a sideways glance, a raised eyebrow, or a one-word comment was enough to send us into gales of laughter. It felt good to know that for an instant we were totally in sync.

We will laugh again, but it will take time and trust to find comparable common ground. Take note when you begin to recover your sense of humor. When you spontaneously burst into laughter, you'll know you've taken another step on the road to recovery.

AFFIRMATION: Slowly I am starting to smile and laugh a little.

*In the last months of his life I had been the target of
his anger.*

                                        —DR. JOYCE BROTHERS

Even as we mourn his absence, we may struggle with feelings
of resentment at having received the brunt of his anger during his illness and death.

Rational explanations are only so helpful here; we know
that when we're in pain, it's natural to lash out at those who
are nearest and dearest, to those we trust to understand and
forgive. We know that—especially if he was heavily medi-
cated—he's not entirely responsible for whatever unpleasant
outbursts may have occurred. When my Papa Phillip was
dying of leukemia, he accused my grandma, Sophie, of having an affair with the czar of Russia; he was convinced of her
adultery; she knew he was hallucinating, and yet she kept
insisting on her innocence.

His angry words may still sting, and for that we must
forgive him. Begin with this exercise:

**AFFIRMATION: It hurt me when you . . .
              I forgive you for . . .**

Just as we needed the opportunity to ask our mate's forgiveness, now we need to forgive *him* for the ways he unwittingly hurt us over the years. One recent wound may be the ways in which we were the target of his anger prior to death. Times he disappointed or betrayed us may leave a reservoir of pain that's difficult to reconcile without his presence.

Here's another option: In the following space write a letter to your love granting him forgiveness. Begin with these words:

My Dearest_____,

    I forgive you for . . .

MONTH FOUR   **DAY TWENTY-THREE**

What soap is for the body, tears are for the soul.
———JEWISH PROVERB

We purify our soul by releasing the floodgates, sobbing and weeping until we're emotionally spent.

We feel strangely peaceful and replenished in the aftermath of a good cry. We're lighter, looser, as if a weight has been lifted off our heart. Which is why it's important to let the tears come, whenever they may. At times we may fight the flood, fearful that we will be overwhelmed with a torrent beyond our control. But if we let the tears come, they will naturally run their course. Resisting them keeps them locked up inside; releasing them has the power of a long, hard thunderstorm. Afterward everything seems fresh and renewed.

AFFIRMATION: My tears are cleansing.

THE DEATHBED

> *"So now you can let go, my darling." He stroked her*
> *gray hair. "Now you can let go."*
>
> —ALDOUS HUXLEY

Some of us have recurring memories of deathbed scenes: I sat by my grandma, Sophie's, bed as she struggled to hold on, giving permission to give up, quietly whispering, "Let go now. Let go."

Unless our spouse died suddenly, the final moments preceding death have a powerful impact. In what may have been one of the most meaningful encounters of our marriage, we said, "Good-bye." We said, "I don't want you to hurt anymore." We said, "Now you can let go, my darling, now you can let go." In that moment of altruistic love we let go, despite our heartbreak, despite our horror at relinquishing our mate.

Our desire to help smooth our mate's transition from this world to the next was a profound act of love. It may be one of the hardest and most generous things we do in our lifetime.

AFFIRMATION: I loved him that much.

MONTH FOUR   **DAY TWENTY-FIVE**

What do I do now that you're gone?

—MOST WIDOWS

We just do what we have to do, slowly but surely putting one foot in front of the other, until we're more solid and secure.

Start with the basics: eating, paying bills, getting to work if you're employed, taking care of business commitments and other daily responsibilities.

The second step may be to tackle death-related issues: notifying the insurance company, corresponding with relevant associations that your husband was a member of, and writing thank-you notes for flowers, letters, and contributions.

Gradually, as we deal with tangible, immediate issues, we're more able to confront the more challenging steps ahead, which will help return us to the land of the living.

AFFIRMATION: I have to start somewhere.

RESENTMENT

I'm sick of listening to how much everyone else misses him!

—RANDI N.

It's a double-edged sword; it's comforting to know that others are affected by our loved one's death, but we resent implications that their suffering is analogous to ours. They may miss him, but it's nothing compared to the magnitude of our loss. At times we're tempted to blurt out, "Your grief doesn't hold a candle to mine!"

How do we graciously acknowledge other people's sadness without lashing out in anger? By remembering these three facts: (a) Every person handles his pain in his own way; (b) this is other people's attempt to reach out and empathize with what we're going through; and (c) our spouse is mourned by others, which is something we can appreciate as a living tribute to how very much he was loved and continues to be missed.

AFFIRMATION: I won't be possessive about my loss.

My mother was dead for five years before I knew that I loved her very much.

—LILLIAN HELLMAN

We've all been told, time and time again, the importance of appreciating what we have. Now these words mean so much more. Even if we consistently loved and adored our spouse, even if we're fully aware of how fortunate we were, his death makes us that much more grateful for how much we truly had.

If our relationship was rocky, we may find our appreciation growing in retrospect. As the months pass, we may find we can forgive him for ways he let us down. In his absence we may rediscover ways in which he was a gift and that perhaps we loved him more than we thought.

This, too, is part of the healing process. We realize how much he meant to us; we let him know, in whatever way makes sense, and once more we say:

AFFIRMATION: I give thanks for the time I had him in my life.

EXTENDED FAMILY

*Funny about families. You think they'll hang together
after a loss. But death doesn't necessarily unite you.*
         —ANNE HOSANSKY

We may have hoped—or fantasized—that our mate's death
would bring us closer to our family, healing past wounds,
uniting us in our shared grief.

Sometimes that's exactly what happens. But unfortunately
we may be sorely disappointed. Family crisis can have the
opposite effect—intensifying conflict and estrangement.

"I had hoped that my husband, Steven's, death would be a
catalyst in my son, Bruce, and I resolving our differences,"
says Barbara, "but instead, right after the funeral, Bruce
accused me of having 'run his father right into the
ground.' " Tamar had a similar experience: Following her
husband's death, her mother-in-law, with whom she'd always fought, refused to speak to her at the cemetery. "I was
ready to forgive and forget," says Tamar. "I thought we
would reach out to each other, but I was wrong."

It's a blessing if our bereavement is an opportunity for
family healing. If it's not possible, turn to sympathetic, supportive relatives and your "family of friends" with whom
you can safely share your grief.

**AFFIRMATION: I am grateful for everyone—relatives
and friends—I can call members of my family.**

Have You Made Peace with Your Husband's Family?

This is one of those loose ends worth tying up. Many of us are fortunate to enjoy loving relationships with our in-laws and the rest of our mate's relatives. But others may have unfinished business in this area—amends to make, conflicts to resolve—and sometimes just the simple act of acknowledging differences will help heal the past and mend fences with your mate's family.

Our healing takes many forms. This is one of the more difficult—and most rewarding—ways we honor our mate.

RESILIENCE

I'm not going to lie down and let trouble walk over me.
—ELLEN GLASGOW

Bravo! Sometimes it's fine to curl up under the covers and sometimes we need to fight! Putting up a good fight doesn't mean that we ignore our troubles or refrain from handling them. It doesn't mean we repress our sadness and act as if everything's just fine. Rather it means we find the resilience to get up, get going, and get things done.

It's all in our attitude. We can be a victim or a victor, which is all measured by the way we choose to conduct ourselves. A victim acts defeated—her troubles get the best of her. A victor picks herself up and says:

AFFIRMATION: I have what it takes to fight the good fight.

At times . . . one is downright thankful for the self-absorption of other people.

—Gail Godwin

Sometimes socializing is a strain, but other times it provides welcome relief from our constant obsession with loss.

There are days when it's nice to immerse ourselves in other people's concerns; babbling about trivial issues can get our mind off ourselves. Not having to talk about death and our adjustment to it can be a reprieve; it can be emotionally exhausting to respond to people's condolences and endlessly give updates on our state of mind.

It is up to us to let other people know if and when it's okay not to focus on our widowhood. Be explicit in inviting them to share the details of their lives. Try these simple, straightforward words:

AFFIRMATION: How are you doing?

MEDICATION

Thank God for sleeping pills.

—JILL TRUMAN

It's a temporary solution, one we must be careful to use in moderation. During the first weeks and months it may make sense to ask your medical provider for a light sleeping pill to help you get through the night. Rest is essential to taking care of business during daylight hours; sleep deprivation increases depression and disorientation, which are part and parcel of grief.

But be careful not to get hooked. Sleeping pills are a last resort, not a quick fix. Try warm milk, a hot bath, relaxation tapes, and reading in bed before resorting to prescription pills.

If you *do* choose sleeping pills, be sure not to mix them with alcohol, and think of them only as a short-term plan. If after six weeks you still turn to them for slumber, consult your physician. It may be time to cut way back or to wean yourself off of them entirely. Ultimately you need to learn how to sleep without him at your side.

AFFIRMATION: I will carefully monitor medication use under a doctor's supervision.

We may uncover shocking correspondences, hidden financial dealings, or romantic betrayals postdeath. This comes as a huge blow. We thought we knew him, now we're not so sure. How are we to cope with the anger, resentment, and loss of trust resulting from such revelations?

If this is irrelevant to your situation, be glad and move on to the next passage. If, however, this is pertinent, take the time to compose a letter, expressing your rage and disappointment. Begin with these words:

My Dearest_____,

    I am devastated by what I've discovered. . . .

*Envy: When I forget that to trade places with another is
simply to trade problems.*

—STEPHANIE ERICCSON

It's human to covet in another that which we long for for
ourselves. Naturally we envy other women whose husbands
are alive; their lives seem perfect in comparison to our own.

But in truth each of us has our own cross to bear. From
the outside looking in, our yearning and loneliness make any
married couple appear blissfully happy. And hopefully they
are. More likely though, their marriage, like ours, has its ups
and downs, periods of chaos, times of serenity.

It's fine to wish for what other women have, so long as
our envy doesn't turn to bitterness, so long as we are careful
to not idealize others or diminish the ways in which our own
lives continue to be full.

AFFIRMATION: I won't waste energy envying others.

"Widow" is a harsh and hurtful word. It comes from the Sanskrit and it means "empty."

—LYNN CAINE

Harsh and hurtful because it implies that something is missing, that the well has run dry, that without our mate our lives are empty and incomplete.

But sorrow doesn't necessarily equal emptiness. Being empty implies nothingness—the absence of feeling, which is the opposite of what occurs during grieving. Although at times we may feel barren—as if nothing will fill the gaping hole in our heart—mostly we are overflowing with emotion, deeply aware of being intensely, painfully alive.

Rather than thinking of our loss as a void that needs to be filled, think of it as an opening, a well in which the water is slowly but surely replenishing itself.

AFFIRMATION: I am overflowing with emotion.

> *Once you have lived with another, it is a great torture*
> *to have to live alone.*
>
> —CARSON MCCULLERS

Not necessarily. Although there's no denying that the shift from cohabitation to living alone is a major life adjustment, there *are* some advantages.

Among them, more time to pursue personal interests and friendships. Making choices—whether it's what to eat for dinner or whether or not to take a vacation—based solely on our own needs and desires. The freedom to come and go as we please, without answering to anyone.

There are trade-offs, to be sure. But whether we find living alone torturous, up and down, or surprisingly pleasant, the fact remains: we didn't choose it, and *that's* the hardest part of all. And we needn't necessarily choose to live alone permanently. At some point down the road we may remarry or find a roommate; or we may discover that living alone, when it's voluntary, has plenty to recommend it.

AFFIRMATION: I don't have to be alone if I don't want to.

When I'm alone, I can sleep crossways in bed without an argument.

—ZSA ZSA GABOR

Being able to sleep crossways or sprawl out, with or without covers, is one tangible benefit of living alone. But like so many aspects of widowhood, it's a mixed blessing. We miss cuddling, sleeping like spoons, cradling our head on his shoulder, listening to his breathing as we blissfully drifted off to sleep.

On the other side we may not miss his chronic snoring, cover snatching, or habit of listening to the ball game while we're trying to read in peace. Before he died, there were nights when we would have loved the luxury of having the bed to ourselves once in a while. Now we'd give up our rest —and more—to hold him in our arms for just one night.

AFFIRMATION: Good night, my prince.

There is no correct way to grieve and no time limit.
—PEGGY EASTMAN

This is one of the most infuriating aspects of grieving; others seem to have a timetable—usually one year—by which time we ought to be over our mourning and on with our lives.

Teresa, who recently marked the first anniversary of her late husband's death, recalls, "As soon as one year had passed, people said things like, 'Now you can date,' which was the farthest thing from my mind."

Rachel, another widow, had a similar experience in which she felt patronized and judged by a passing comment. "Despite what rough shape I was in, I had forced myself to go to my best friend's birthday party three months after Jake died," she says, "and this person I barely knew came up to me and asked, 'Isn't it a little soon to be partying?'!"

These sorts of unsolicited comments are misguided at best, rude and unacceptable judgments coming from someone who doesn't have a clue as to what we're going through and how best to endure it. Each of us grieves in our own way, at our own personal pace. There is no one way, no right way, only the way that best facilitates our healing.

AFFIRMATION: Accept me. Don't judge me.

You know you're healing when you're familiar with the tool kit.

—ANNE HOSANSKY

Either that or you may simply be desperate enough to figure out how to use a wrench because it's the only way to fix the broken lock on the door.

Whether motivated by necessity or choice, learning to take on new responsibilities that were previously part of *his* job description is another way of making peace with the present. Whether it's figuring out how to hang a picture, change a tire, or shovel the walk, it's all a matter of broadening our abilities to cope with the practicalities of living on our own.

Of course, depending on our financial status, there's always an option of paying for services, particularly those we find unwieldy or downright beyond our ken. Hiring help is fine, but knowing we can do it ourselves does wonders for our sense of mastery and independence. It makes us feel stronger and more confident that we can handle whatever comes our way.

AFFIRMATION: I can do it.

Have You Taken
Your Car for a Tune-up?

We can substitute any or all of the following: taken your tax returns to the accountant, taken your winter clothes out of storage, taken your cat to the vet, or just about any other necessary task that may have been on his list, which has now been added to yours.

Start tackling these projects by making a short list of responsibilities you've been avoiding and are ready to take on. Then pick one and do it. Then another. And another.

*Self-pity in its early stages is as snug as a feather bed.
Only when it hardens does it become uncomfortable.*
                                        —MAYA ANGELOU

There is a fine line between sorrow and self-pity, between releasing tears and drowning in them, between nursing wounds and doing the necessary grieving that ultimately leads to healing.

How do we know the difference? Sorrow is a temporary response to a specific situation. Self-pity is an ongoing attitude that permeates our lives, regardless of our situation. Sorrow welcomes comfort; self-pity pushes others away. Sorrow says, "I hurt." Self-pity says, "Poor me."

A certain measure of sorrow comes with the territory of loss. Self-pity, too, is natural, so long as it doesn't become the guiding principle, the overall way in which we relate to ourselves and others. We can feel our pain without being governed by it.

AFFIRMATION: I won't wallow in self-pity.

> *I suppose a sudden death may seem "appealing" to those
> who have suffered through a husband's long terminal
> illness, but losing him unexpectedly is like a punch in
> the solar plexus.*
>
> —PHILOMENE GATES

It's six of one, half a dozen of the other, and neither's a bargain.

Women who have watched their spouses suffer a long, agonizing death are drained by the experience. On the positive side—if there's a positive side—we've had time to prepare ourselves emotionally and financially, as well as the chance to complete unfinished business and gradually say good-bye.

Sudden death, in contrast, comes as a huge shock to our system. One moment everything's fine, then suddenly our lives are in shambles. It takes a long time to believe what's happening is real; it may take even longer to come to terms with all the things we wish we'd said but never had the chance.

As widows we need to fight the temptation to play the my-tragedy-is-more-tragic-than-yours game. Each of us has suffered in our own way. Each of us deserves compassion and respect.

AFFIRMATION: Everyone has his or her own cross to bear. I will try to be compassionate.

MONTH FIVE   DAY THIRTEEN

*How did a person survive without intimacy? Didn't you
need at least one person in the world to know who you
really were?*

—JUDITH FREEMAN

Yes. And perhaps far more than one, but in many different
ways.

We have lost the exquisite, unspoken understanding that
bonded us with our beloved. It took years to build the trust
and intimacy that allowed us to be who we really are, without pretense, without fear of rejection. We felt loved for
ourselves, in all our imperfection, and that was an incompa-
rable treasure.

We may hesitate to become close, armoring ourselves as a
way of preventing further hurt and abandonment. But love is
essential. We must work a little harder to create and sustain
different sorts of intimacy—with our children, our friends,
and perhaps eventually a new romantic partner. Human
touch, a voice calling out, "How are you? Are you doing
okay?" knowing there are other human beings holding you in
their hearts, will make a world of difference in the days
ahead.

AFFIRMATION: I will slowly begin to let others in.

BOUNDARIES

Where does one person end and another person begin?
                                                —IRIS MURDOCH

"It's as if part of me has been amputated," says Nan, a widow of three months, describing a palpable sense of being physically and psychically cut off.

Even as we were two separate individuals, in many ways we felt like one—our unity reflected in the merger of our beings. We'd start a sentence, he'd finish it. Lying in bed, making love with our fingers intertwined, feeling perfectly, blissfully, fluidly in sync, at times it was as if we weren't certain where one began and the other ended.

Now we are left standing alone. We reach for his comforting presence, longing for reunion, just once more to be as one.

AFFIRMATION: You will always be a part of me.

*I wanted to die too. I felt as if my future had been
wiped out along with his.*

—PHILOMENE GATES

Feeling suicidal is a common—and understandable—response to a loss of this magnitude. At first we wonder if there's any point to going on. Life seems empty. Meaningless. The future—a golden vision of shared hopes and dreams—now seems a cruel joke. Not only have we been robbed of the present, but tomorrow—and all the tomorrows to follow—are a formidable question mark that fills us with apprehension.

These are powerful feelings. And they are temporary feelings. The future—as we planned it—has changed: we need to grieve the disintegration of our dreams in order to reconcile reality. At the same time, we must go on. We must summon our life force, tapping our deepest resources of courage and hope, even in the midst of mourning our loss.

It takes time—and lots of it—to believe that life will again be sweet. If suicidal thoughts are daily, obsessive demons, seek professional help. If occasionally you fall into the depths, not to worry. Trust that with each passing day it gets easier and easier to look forward to tomorrow.

AFFIRMATION: The sun will come out tomorrow.

*I have not moved the eyeglasses from the table next to
our bed.*

—Ruth Coughlin

Some widows leave everything exactly as it was: the loose
change in his wallet, his pills on the bathroom counter, the
robe he left draped over a chair the last time he was home
from the hospital. It can be deeply comforting to surround
ourselves with his personal items for a while, as a way of
holding him close.

Other women find it extremely healing to carefully put
away their spouse's belongings, even rearranging their bedroom to make it more comfortable in the present. Either
way is right if it's right for you. As long as leaving things as
they are isn't a way of remaining paralyzed in pain, make
each symbolic move as you're emotionally ready for it.

**AFFIRMATION: I will let go of my beloved at my own
pace.**

You know you're healing when you introduce yourself without saying in the next breath, "I've lost my husband."

—ANNE HOSANSKY

It takes time. In the beginning it's the first words out of our mouth; we're absorbed with his death and we can't stop talking about it to anyone and everyone.

Gradually our widowhood becomes less and less our primary focus. We're able to carry on a conversation without drifting off or becoming impatient. We're able to concentrate on worldly issues and care about the details of other people's lives. Most important we aren't compelled to let every person we encounter in on the intimate details of our grief.

Which isn't to say that we should inhibit or censor ourselves with those we love and trust. Saying "I've lost my husband"—as many times as we need—out loud or to ourselves is a way of coming to terms with reality, a necessary part of the healing process. Little by little we need to say it less and less.

AFFIRMATION: My husband's death is a primary—yet not the only—driving force in my life.

The coronary death rate among widows aged twenty-five to thirty-five is five times that of married women in the same age group.
— NATIONAL BUREAU OF STATISTICS

This frightening statistic speaks volumes about the level of emotional and physiological connection between ourselves and our loved one. And it serves as an important reminder of the vital importance of taking very, very good care of ourselves.

Any life crisis—especially one involving a loss of this magnitude—creates vulnerability. Our susceptibility to illness is increased from lost sleep, skipped meals, and an overall tendency to stop exercising and caring for ourselves. Conversely we're at higher risk for smoking, alcohol and chemical abuse, and other addictive behaviors as a way of medicating depression.

We've all heard tragic stories of widows who died ''of a broken heart'' following their spouse's death. As our hearts are healing, it's vitally important to do everything possible to stay physically fit. With time, life *will* seem worth living; until it does, we need to make every effort, as hard as it may be, to remain healthy and strong.

AFFIRMATION: I want to live.

Are You Getting Any Exercise?

Regular exercise is one of the best antidotes for depression. Any consistent workout, whether we join a health club or take a brisk lap around the block, has numerous rewards: We feel better. We make an investment in our physical and mental health. And especially if we exercise at a club, there is the added social benefit, even if it's as minimal as exchanging sympathetic smiles while we're sweating on the StairMaster.

And there's another plus: Regular commitments we make help us stay focused and prevent isolation. If there's only one thing you do for yourself right now, this would be a great first step.

> *As a widow I found myself directly in the middle of*
> *foreign territory: another generation's principles, values*
> *and beliefs.*
>
> —XENIA ROSE

Never has the so-called generation gap had such a personal impact, particularly when it comes to dating. The rules of the game have changed, and we feel like relics—out of touch and ill at ease about how to conduct ourselves.

Are we to wait for invitations (most women grew up believing it was the man's place to call) or do we pick up the phone and ask *him* on a date? Who pays? Who drives? And most importantly is sex as easy and casual as some of our daughters would have us believe?

The last thing we want is to seem old-fashioned and stodgy. By the same token we mustn't compromise our values. We can only stretch so far; through trial and error we discover our limits and how far we can venture beyond our comfort zone.

As usual the best advice is: When in doubt, don't. Anyone who is put off by your unwillingness to put out doesn't merit your company. A man who respects your integrity is well worth the wait.

AFFIRMATION: I am who I am. No apologies.

CREDIT

MONTH FIVE   **DAY TWENTY-ONE**

*Then came another blow. Visa shredded my card and
said I had ceased to exist.*

—XENIA ROSE

Ouch! Talk about adding insult to injury! Just when we're
feeling most vulnerable, we're struck by another blow. Some
nameless, faceless voice over the phone informs us we've
been cut off. It's a major blow to our personhood *and* our
pocketbook.

This is another example of twenty-twenty hindsight. Why
didn't we make contingency plans, establishing credit in our
own name so that this crisis could be avoided?

The fact is, we just didn't. Many, many widows, as a
matter of course and convention, were covered under their
spouse's credit, but not as primary card holders. None of
which makes us stupid, simply victims of an era in which it
didn't occur to us to do otherwise.

Now, however, it's time to take action. Intimidating—and
humiliating—as it may be, it's essential to get credit in your
own name. Where to begin? Here are some tried-and-true
tips:

- Find out what collateral you have (your home, checking
  and savings accounts, personal valuables) that can be
  used to secure credit.
- Take out a small loan and pay it back as soon as possible.
- Rather than starting out with a major credit card, begin
  with a local department store, so that you can build a
  positive credit rating.

The sooner you take care of business, the more peace of
mind you'll have. It's a worthwhile investment.

**AFFIRMATION: I'm ready to take responsibility for my
finances.**

Have You Made a Living Will?

Whether your mate did or didn't have a living will, his death is a good reminder for you to take care of this important piece of business for yourself. A living will is useful for three reasons: (a) in order for your wishes to be honored, they must be clarified in writing; (b) it relieves your children and other loved ones of having to make difficult decisions down the road; and (c) it's another way of taking personal responsibility for the duration of your life. Your medical provider can direct you in how to proceed.

If you can't change your fate, change your attitude.
                                    —AMY TAN

We had no choice over being widowed; we do, however, have the power to choose our attitude. Mourning often leads to depression; it's easy to sink into a "cup half empty" frame of mind.

Making a concious decision to embrace a positive attitude, to choose self-empowerment over self-pity, can profoundly affect our experience. Instead of saying, "I'm all alone," we can say, "I have myself, my friends, my children." Instead of saying, "It's not fair that he died," we can say, "Thank God we had so many wonderful years together."

This is not about being "Pollyanna," denying our sadness and putting on a happy face. Rather, it's about putting the best spin on our circumstances by holding on to optimism and hope.

AFFIRMATION: My attitude is 100 percent up to me.

There are moments when I would like to tell people that until you experience a loss this big, everything else is amateur night.

—RUTH COUGHLIN

It's incredibly frustrating to listen to other people's relatively superficial woes: their car's broken down; they're having trouble with their boss; they can't get their husband to pick up his socks (which makes you want to scream, "What the hell are you complaining about, just be glad he's alive!").

This is a real dilemma, without any simple answers, just these two truths: First, there is no comparing trivial day-to-day aggravations with the dramatic loss you've sustained. Second, in every person's life there are ups and downs, which for them pose a serious challenge, regardless of how much they pale in comparison to ours.

Which leaves you with two choices: You can erupt, outraged that anyone would dare to burden you with their troubles in the midst of your trauma. Or you can try to be tolerant and understanding, lending the wisdom of your experience to helping others rise to the occasion.

AFFIRMATION: I'll try to be tolerant of other people's problems.

When one is pretending, the entire body revolts.
                                                —ANAÏS NIN

It's exhausting and stressful to keep up pretenses, to "put on a happy face" when inside we're falling apart. To whatever degree possible, avoid situations in which you have to pretend to be anything other than you are. Spend time with friends who are comfortable with your pain. Be as open as possible with your co-workers, explaining that you are in crisis, that it may be a long time before your life is back in balance. If going to parties or other social events pressures you to be "up," choose other ways to fill your time, ways that will allow you to be as shaky as you feel.

There is no timetable. There is no reason to pretend. You get to be who you are—in all your pain—until you're genuinely in a new and different place.

AFFIRMATION: I needn't keep a stiff upper lip.

One of the basic tenets of the spiritual seeker is: My life is a classroom. I am learning an important lesson from this experience.

—MARY HAYES-GRIECO

It's natural to feel angry and bitter, to ask, "Why did this have to happen to me?"

But as Rabbi Harold Kushner, in his book *When Bad Things Happen to Good People,* points out, if I say, "Why did this have to happen to me?" then I must also be willing to ask, "Why am I so lucky?"

In the midst of our pain, it's hard to see the lessons. Yet they are abundant. Whereas we certainly didn't "sign up" for this difficult and challenging course, it has been a learning experience. One widow, Teresa, says, "I've learned—the hard way—how to take care of myself." Another widow, Rhoda, says, "I'm much more compassionate with regard to other people's pain."

If possible, take a moment to evaluate the lessons you're learning—and continue to learn—as a result of all you've been through.

AFFIRMATION: I'm learning_____

*You know you are healing when you automatically say
"I" instead of "We."*

—ANNE HOSANSKY

It can take a long time to make the shift from saying *we* to
saying *I*. We're accustomed to thinking of ourselves as part
of a pair. It's second nature to think and respond in the
plural; without realizing, we say, "We'd love to come to the
party," "We have five grandchildren," "We've been working on cutting fat out of our diet."

Every time we remember to say *I* rather than *we*, we are
reminded of our loss, once again shocked into the recognition that we are alone, which is both terrifying and exciting.
The security of We is traded for the independence of I. For
better or for worse, we slowly get used to being absolutely
on our own.

AFFIRMATION: I am still getting used to I.

Expect your judgment to be clouded.
—HAROLD BLOOMFIELD AND PETER MCWILLIAMS

Feeling disoriented, cloudy, and unable to make clear, sound decisions are typical manifestations of grieving. We may feel as if we're walking around in a fog. We may have trouble forming a thought, articulating our feelings, making even the most trivial of choices, such as what to eat, what TV show to watch, whether to wear the brown shoes or the black.

None of which means we're losing our minds, although it can certainly feel that way in the early stages of grieving. It's as if our entire system has a short in it; the circuits aren't connecting and we can't quite seem to throw the right switch.

What we *can* do, as the authors of *How to Survive the Loss of a Love* point out, is to be prepared. If we expect to be at less than capacity, if we can be patient with ourselves and adjust our expectations, our clarity and powers of discernment will gradually return.

AFFIRMATION: My confusion is a natural response to crisis.

> *Another surprise was learning to enjoy the company of*
> *my women friends for themselves and not as "poor sub-*
> *stitutes" for men.*
>
> —PHILOMENE GATES

Most of us have been raised to feel as if we must be with a man to be complete, as if women friends, however loved, however valued, take second fiddle to romance and intimacy.

As we get older, we discover the precious friendships of women are not poor substitutes for men, but wonderfully satisfying relationships in their own right.

Time spent with my women friends is priceless to me; long gone are the days when I would break plans with women for a date with a man. With my women friends I can be totally myself. Their support, empathy, and capacity for nurturing far exceeds what most men have to offer.

Which is not to say that men are expendable, only that learning to appreciate the company of women is a gift and a blessing.

AFFIRMATION: Thank God for the women in my life.

To love a person means to agree to grow old with him.
—ANONYMOUS

It feels like a broken promise; we had fantasies of stroking his gray beard, admiring our great-grandchildren, tenderly reminiscing as we enjoyed the golden years of our lives.

We knew there was no guarantee, but it hurts all the same. We can rue the fact that we will never grow old with him, or we can count all the years—all the life stages—we were fortunate to share: the experience of raising children, building careers, traveling, celebrating graduations and weddings, perhaps even years of retirement when we had the leisure to enjoy one another's company, free of work, financial stress, and other encumbrances of earlier times.

We will never grow old together—but we certainly have grown through whatever days we had. Through this portion of our journey we were lucky to have him by our side.

AFFIRMATION: I grieve not being able to grow old with you at my side.

We are accustomed to sharing our friendships with our spouse; we always enjoyed letting him know who was important in our lives and why they mattered so very much.

As widows our friendships are changing and evolving. In the following space write a letter to your love describing the most meaningful relationships in your life right now. Begin with these words:

My Dearest_____,

My most sustaining friendships at present are . . .

Medgar constantly prepared me to be able to live and achieve without him.

                                 —MYRLIE EVERS

At times we may have resented our husband's insistence on our self-reliance: when he insisted we learn how to balance the checkbook, learn how to put up the storm windows, get the oil changed when he could just as easily have done it himself. If his death followed a long illness, he might have been especially adamant about pushing us to master new skills, which may have aroused our resistance. We knew we'd have to cope on our own, but preparing for it simply drove home the reality of his impending death.

Now we can thank him for the ways in which he nurtured our independence. We know we can take care of business. But we still wish he was here to take care of us—not because we can't do it ourselves but because we miss him so.

AFFIRMATION: Thank you for helping me prepare for the inevitable.

A woman in one of my widow groups sat up straight in her chair and quietly but firmly said, "I can't identify with the rest of you, because frankly I had a lousy marriage, and I'm glad he's gone."

—LYNN CAINE

Okay, here's the other side, and it's not very pretty.

There are women among us for whom widowhood is a welcome relief from an unrelentingly unhappy marriage. This extreme example is the exception, not the norm; most of us fall somewhere in the middle of the spectrum, with the good significantly outweighing the bad.

If you *do* relate to the sentiments above, give yourself credit for your honesty and candor. And give yourself time to see if your feelings soften somewhat, making room for a more positive and forgiving perspective on your relationship.

If such a statement makes you want to sit up straight in your chair and loudly say, "How dare you? I'd give anything to have my husband back!" try to exercise tolerance and compassion. And be grateful that for you loss is at best bittersweet.

AFFIRMATION: I understand.

I can't believe at sixty-two I'm forced to persuade some strange man that I'm sexy and appealing.

—SUZANNE C.

You're not forced! For that matter, let *him* impress *you* rather than worrying about whether you're knocking his socks off.

I know. Easier said than done. Dating, especially after years and years of marriage, is weird, at the very least. For so long we've felt secure in our spouse's love; despite our stretch marks, sagging chins, and extra pounds, we were long past having to seduce our mate or sell him on our attractiveness.

Now we may feel scrutinized, insecure in our ability to attract men. On top of which we resent being in this position, which only makes it worse.

The antidote lies in our own inner confidence, in the capacity to see ourselves as a beautiful, desirable, perfectly "whole" woman with or without a man. We're freer to enjoy men as friends—and perhaps prospective suitors—when we can say:

AFFIRMATION: I don't have to impress anyone. I'm fine just as I am.

So you think you might be falling in love—or lust—with another man. Or perhaps you're mulling over the idea of dating. Or maybe you just smiled at a nice-looking stranger over the carrots at the farmers' market and now you're feeling like a heel.

Whether we're open to romance, ambivalent, or simply occasionally fantasize, it's natural to feel weirdly disloyal to our spouse. We can't help but worry about his feelings, which is why it helps to ask his permission (blessing) for whatever stage we find ourselves in. Begin with these words:

My Dearest_____,

This feels awkward, but I need you to know that . . .

I make an effort not to be an "old mom" waiting to be invited over.

—ANONYMOUS

It's natural to feel more dependent on our grown children; after all, they share our loss in a way no one else can quite relate to, *and* they fill the void at times when we're lonely and need a place to go.

At the same time, we're fearful of acting needy or imposing ourselves on our children. After all, they have their own lives, their own work, their own children; we don't want to be a burden on their already busy schedules.

There's a fine line between overdependence on our children and remaining aloof. An honest conversation is one way to set boundaries and make sure you're not wearing out your welcome. Another way to be sure of staying on the right side of the line is to work on developing other relationships so that our children aren't our only option. The fuller our own lives are, the better we feel about asking them to dinner or dropping in for a visit.

The need to see them will subside over time. Gradually we're less dependent and more comfortable in our own company.

AFFIRMATION: In some ways this is a brand-new relationship, in which boundaries will become clearer over time.

Some of us—whose role was to cook for, to care for, to be with our mate—may mourn the loss of the purpose of our existence.

—JUDITH VIORST

Having someone to care for fills a profound human need. Before, our identity was defined—at least in part—by all the ways in which our now-departed mate depended on us for support and sustenance. Women whose primary role was as wife may feel especially at loose ends, our sense of purpose and meaning no longer crystal clear as we flounder to redefine ourselves in the present.

We may find comfort within other relationships where we are needed—with our children, our friends, and our community. We may also take this opportunity to learn a little about taking—about letting others cook for, care for, and be with us in whatever ways bring solace. And as we both nurture and let ourselves be replenished, we begin to discover who we are becoming.

AFFIRMATION: I'm still needed, just in different ways.

COURAGE

The only courage that matters is the kind that gets you
from one moment to the next.
                                        —MIGNON MCLAUGHLIN

It's the tried-and-true AA wisdom, and it works. One day at
a time, one hour at a time, sometimes one moment at a time
is all we can face, and it's enough. We needn't be all the way
there; little by little we become stronger, more able to cope,
more confident and willing to move forward in our lives.

It's up and down. After a while entire days pass smoothly
without any emotional outbursts. Other days we awake in
pain, struggling to get through each moment without breaking down.

Getting through the moments, the hours, the days, the
months, takes courage. And faith that, one day at a time, this
will become easier and easier.

AFFIRMATION: It's the small steps that count.

I am incapable of sleeping in our bed, the bed in which there were good times and bad times, the bed in which Bill died.

—RUTH COUGHLIN

It's common for women to avoid sleeping in their bed for a while. His absence is palpable; we toss and turn, holding on to his pillow, trying to find a comfortable position in what feels like a vast wasteland without him at our side.

If our bed was his deathbed, we may hesitate to crawl in. Feelings of sadness, weirdness, fear, and trepidation may keep our bed from being the safe haven it used to be.

For some women the "marriage bed" is a place of sweetness and comfort, full of wonderful memories. For others it may take some time to be able to return to it. Slumber is essential to healing. So sleep wherever you will get the best rest right now.

AFFIRMATION: Sweet dreams.

MEMORIES

*You have to get used to being the only one left who
remembers.*

—PHILOMENE GATES

The older we are, the more years we've had together, the
more memories there are that only belong to the two of us:
our first date, when he was so nervous, he forgot to bring
his wallet. The day our youngest child was born. The hard
times—when we scraped together quarters from the piggy
bank to pay for groceries; the incomparably wonderful times
—cuddling at a north-woods cabin, toasting our marriage in
front of a crackling fire.

Preserving our memories is now part of the sacred trust
remaining to us. We commit to cherish, protect, and remember the shared moments of our love.

AFFIRMATION: I'll never forget you.

How true it is that so many of our memories can only be shared with our beloved. We can recall happy—and not-so-happy—events, trying to convey their meaning to others, but in the final analysis only our spouse completely shared in so many memorable and intimate moments.

Take time now to travel down memory lane, writing a letter of reminiscences. You may laugh, you may cry, but you will surely recall a wealth of shared experiences as you begin with these words:

My Dearest_____,

   Do you remember when . . .

I am glad that I shall not see you old, Love. And you won't see me old and ugly, will you?

—JILL TRUMAN

If we are widowed at a relatively young age, we will never grow old with our beloved, which I suppose falls into the "silver lining" category. As Jill Truman, whose youngest was ten months when her husband died, writes in her memoir, *Letters to My Husband,* "Now I shall sink into middle and old age alone, while you will remain always young."

There is something romantic about remembering our mate in the prime of his life. But there is something equally romantic about having grown old together, having seen one another through the wrinkles of time, love that grew beyond the springtime of our youth.

We will always be grateful for the times together when we were young and sprightly and full of life. And those of us who were fortunate to have more time will cherish the ways in which our love endured.

AFFIRMATION: We had so many good years together.

If you have any notion of where you are going, you will never get anywhere.

—TONI MORRISON

Our spouse's death may have left us feeling lost and directionless. Setting goals, making plans, mapping out our life's itinerary gives us a sense of purpose and control. Wanting a clear and exact map of the future is one way of coping with chaos. We crave the security of knowing where we're going; if only we were sure what the future holds!

It's important to find the right balance between creating a rigid vision—from which we are afraid to veer—and remaining open to unforeseen twists and turns along the road. Being widowed has taught us that life is unpredictable. We have learned that the best-laid plans are always subject to change.

AFFIRMATION: I am learning to be more flexible.

What New Goals Are You Committed To?

There's a fine line between setting reasonable goals and locking ourselves in. We can begin thinking about where we want to be and what we hope to accomplish, leaving ourselves enough room to be flexible and open to change.

Start by completing this exercise: In the following space finish these sentences:

My one-month goal is_____.
My one-year goal is_____.
My five-year goal is_____.

MONTH SIX   **DAY FIFTEEN**

*How dare the sun shine and the flowers bloom and the
garden be beautiful when my love is dead?*
                                              —REBECCA RICE

In the earliest stages of grief we're astounded—even of-
fended—by that fact that life goes on. The mail is delivered,
the state fair opens, neighborhood children board the school
bus as if nothing has happened. Anything that symbolizes
growth can be especially hard to take: people laughing, sunshine pouring down, an invitation to a friend's baby naming
stun us into recognition that, despite our pain, the rest of the
world is carrying on as before.

This is both a comforting and an infuriating paradox: Everything beautiful and alive is in stunning contrast to the
death we've experienced. At the same time it is only through
awareness and appreciation of life that we heal and become
whole.

AFFIRMATION: Life goes on.

> *I should have a big "W" sewn on my chest with an explanation below: "Please be patient. I am recently widowed and cannot remember, plan or think."*
> —DR. ALLA RENEE BOZARTH

Wouldn't it be wonderful if people could read our minds? If they could automatically know what we're going through and instinctively sense how much patience, caring, and understanding we need right now?

Short of wearing a big *W* on our chest, we can't rely on other people to realize how hard it is to stay focused, to handle even the most basic of tasks, to think about much of anything other than our loss. We have to be willing to tell them. It needn't take lengthy explanations, we can simply say, "Please be patient with me. I'm having a hard time."

Anyone who loves you will give you lots of rope. Anyone who expects more of you right now isn't worth your time.

AFFIRMATION: Please, be patient with me.

As time passes, we become more aware of how our mate enhanced the quality of our life. We have so much to thank him for. Only in retrospect can we fully appreciate the numerous ways he supported, strengthened, and cared for us through the years.

In the following space take the opportunity to express your gratitude with these words:

My Dearest_____,

Thank you for . . .

> *Malcolm is gone and Martin is gone and it is up to all
> of us to nourish the hope they gave us.*
> —LENA HORNE

Lena Horne is referring to the profound legacy given us by
Malcolm X and Martin Luther King, Jr., following their
deaths.

We honor their memory by carrying out their vision. So,
too, we are obligated to fulfill our mate's legacy—by doing
everything possible to raise our children well, by completing,
continuing, or, in some cases, simply respecting our spouse's
life work or dedication to causes. Mostly we nourish the
hope we were given by living up to the ways in which our
spouse encouraged and nurtured us. He always bragged
about how sociable we were, now we must remember to
reach out for friendship and companionship. He pushed us to
pursue our art, which we dedicate to him now in his memory. His positive attitude inspired everyone he came in contact with; we try to embody it even in the midst of grieving.

Malcolm is gone. Martin is gone. Our beloved is gone.
But none are forgotten.

AFFIRMATION: You will never be forgotten.

Have You Considered Establishing a Memorial in His Name?

One widow, Eleanor, honored her husband, David's, memory by dedicating a classroom at their church. Marcy, whose husband, Mark, died of cancer, worked with the American Cancer Society to create a special research fund in his name. Susan, whose husband, Travis, was a tenured professor in mathematics, put her energy into establishing a scholarship fund for local youth as a way of continuing her husband's life work.

It's a wonderful way of memorializing our mate. We heal ourselves by helping someone else.

*My daughter's wedding was one of the hardest days of
my life.*

—RITA W.

Finding a way to get through happy occasions—especially
those related to shared passages—remains one of the most
bittersweet challenges of widowhood.

Celebrating our children's milestones is especially difficult. The one person uniquely capable of sharing and appreciating our joy is absent. We sit alone at our son's college
graduation bursting with pride, wanting to grasp his father's
hand. Our hearts ache watching our daughter walk down the
aisle on the arm of someone other than her Dad. We hold
our first grandchild wishing desperately his grandfather could
have lived to see this day.

Our joy is mixed with sorrow, and that's just the way it
should be. These moments, in all their glory, make us deeply
aware of our loss.

AFFIRMATION: My joy is mixed with my sorrow.

In fact, death is a friend who brings deliverance from suffering.

—MAHATMA GANDHI

This is one of the few silver linings worth remembering. As Gandhi wisely says, especially if your spouse endured a long illness, death provides relief—a blessed deliverance from the depths of suffering.

And we are delivered from the anguish of helplessly witnessing our beloved's anguish. We may have uttered the words "Enough already!" or prayed, "Please God, just let him be out of pain."

And so he is. No more invasive tests or excruciating waits between painkillers. No more wishing there was something we could do.

His suffering is over. It's a small comfort—but a real one.

AFFIRMATION: I'm glad his suffering is over.

Each morning I wake up and say, "Dear Lord, I don't want anything better; just send me more of the same."
—KITTY CARLISLE HART

We were happy with what we had; we'd put lots of effort into our marriage and were enjoying the fruits of our labor. We'd achieved a certain level of comfort, trust, and companionship, for which we were abundantly grateful.

Now we're not even sure what to hope and pray for. So here are a few suggestions: We pray for our lives to gradually resume some measure of order and peace. We pray for the courage to get through each day without falling apart. We pray that in time we will again feel joy and happiness, that we will be able to wake in the morning and say:

AFFIRMATION: Just send me more of the same.

I didn't know how to be mother and father to my children.

—ALEXANDRA B.

And we needn't be, although we may feel compelled to do double duty, to make up for the missing father our children so sorely miss.

We can only be responsible mothers, which means allowing our children their pain and keeping their father's memory alive. We can't replace him; it isn't up to us to compensate for his absence.

Although no one will ever be their father, we *can,* when appropriate, invite other men into our children's lives, as friends, guides, and mentors. A favorite uncle or family friend can offer some of the "daddy love" that complements all the many ways we're mom.

AFFIRMATION: I only have to be the mother.

Unless we never had children, we may desperately miss the opportunity to share day-to-day parenting trials and triumphs, as well as our sons' and daughters' milestones. We can regale our friends with stories about our children's accomplishments, but it's just not the same; we may worry about bragging or boring them with details that only our husband would appreciate. In the following space write your beloved a letter telling him how the children are doing:

My Dearest_____,

Let me bring you up to date on the children. . . .

Not only is physical pain more acceptable than emotional pain in most families, it gets more positive attention.
— Dr. Alla Renee Bozarth

Which may be one of the reasons our grief takes the form of physical illness. Most of us were raised in families ill equipped to communicate about and cope with emotional pain. Whereas our parents automatically called the doctor when we had the flu, few sought out counseling unless precipitated by a crisis, and even then they may have kept their feelings to themselves.

We may have internalized messages that promote stoicism, that prevent our capacity to share our pain for fear of seeming weak or needy. Plus there's the added fear of making others uncomfortable. If we complain of a headache, they can rush to our rescue with Advil, but they're helpless to fix our emotional anguish.

It's time to stop judging our feelings and it's time to stop worrying about whether they're too intense for others to deal with. Right now our only task is to heal.

AFFIRMATION: I needn't be ashamed of feeling lousy.

Love makes us poets and the approach of death should make us philosophers.

—GEORGE SANTAYANA

In other words the experience of death should motivate us to ask questions about the meaning of life.

We seek a philosophical framework that will help us reconcile our mate's death. We may become more introspective, musing about fate's place in our circumstances, the possibility of an afterlife, exploring metaphysical theories in order to comprehend the incomprehensible, to make sense of tragedy as a way of finding peace.

The search for meaning—for a cosmic justification for our loss—is part of the process of coming to terms with our loss. Answers may or may not be forthcoming, but the questions themselves bring us closer to accepting our loss.

AFFIRMATION: It's asking the questions that counts.

The word "widow" weighs me down. Men joke that they better be careful not to marry me if that is my luck with men.

— STEPHANIE ERICCSON

The first time I confided to a prospective date that my ex-husband was gay, he said, "What did you do to drive him to *that*?"

Needless to say, I didn't give this person the time of day. But nevertheless his words stung. Even though I knew he was kidding (or at worst so uncomfortable with the conversation he couldn't help but put his foot in his mouth), I still felt defensive, as if somehow my value as a woman was diminished by a situation over which I had no control.

Likewise widows are subject to insensitive comments and not-very-funny jokes—people's clumsy attempt at coping with death. When this happens, we have two choices: We can gently, but firmly set the record straight, or we can walk away, repeating to ourselves:

AFFIRMATION: This isn't about me. I don't have to take it on.

> *A friend told me that every time she saw her mother-in-law, she found herself taking a backseat as the woman listed her agonies over losing a son.*
>
> —XENIA ROSE

We feel possessive in our grief, as if no one, including our children or our deceased husband's parents, can possibly come close to feeling the anguish of our loss. We may even resent their expressions of pain: we have enough to cope with without attending to their needs.

Of course we *aren't* the only one affected by our spouse's death: our children are deeply aggrieved; our in-laws surely agonize through the profound loss of their beloved child. We can reach out to one another as long as we don't drain our energies or become distracted by dealing with other family members' mourning. First we must concentrate on healing ourselves. Then we can focus on the task of witnessing and attending to the suffering of our loved ones.

AFFIRMATION: There is plenty of suffering to go around.

MONTH SIX   **DAY TWENTY-NINE**

Grief itself is a medicine.

—WILLIAM COWPER

Like most medicines it tastes bitter, but it is necessary in order to resume health and well-being.

Medicine takes a while to have an effect; its effectiveness is dependent on our willingness to diligently participate in the process, to patiently allow it to flow through our system, and to facilitate its capacity to heal by getting lots of rest while it works its magic.

And we notice that, like most medicines, grief's curative powers build gradually; it is a subtle process, one that happens almost without our noticing. Each day we realize our grief is diminishing and we feel a little bit better than the day before.

AFFIRMATION: I am swallowing my medicine.

> *It's not the length but the quality of life that matters to me.*
>
> —JANE RULE

Ultimately it's not how long we live but what we make of the time we have on this earth.

No matter what age our mate was when he died, we may feel angry that his time was abbreviated. It helps to concentrate instead on the positive aspects of his existence—on all the relationships he fostered, the work he accomplished, the wisdom he accrued, the meaningful and joyous experiences that defined the quality of his life.

Rereading the eulogy is one way to focus on quality rather than quantity, to remember that what matters is to live fully, for whatever time we have.

AFFIRMATION: My husband made the most of his days.

MONTH SEVEN   **DAY ONE**

I live a life that pleases me.

—OLIVIA DE HAVILLAND

One benefit widowhood offers is greater personal freedom and independence. We have only ourselves to please; little things such as what to have for dinner, and big decisions such as where to live, how to spend our money, what friendships to engage in, and what community and spiritual engagements to pursue are now strictly our own, and we are likely to feel ambivalent about this.

On the one hand we miss our mate's counsel. We trusted his judgment and enjoyed the mutuality of joint decision making. And we may greatly miss the joy of taking another human being's opinions into account, of going out of our way to please him.

On the other hand it's our turn to concentrate on ourselves. We get to be selfish, we get to live a life based on our desires, our needs, defining what makes us happy, which challenges us to know ourselves well and take risks on our own behalf.

AFFIRMATION: It's time to figure out what pleases me.

Accepting our loss also means accepting that he is no longer part of our future—he will miss sharing with us the ways in which we are growing and changing, and we will miss being able to depend on him as a sounding board and support as we continue to evaluate our beliefs, priorities, and goals.

But we can keep him posted. In the space below write a letter updating your mate on the ways in which you are evolving. Tell him about new viewpoints, changing values, and emerging ambitions that have come about since his death:

My Dearest_____,

Since your death, here are some of the ways in which I have started to change: . . .

Life is a journey and death is a destination.

—TORAH

"I was angry that I didn't have any control over the journey Bob and I were on," says Wendy, whose husband died of a heart attack at forty-two. "We'd made well-thought-out plans, we'd charted our destiny, then boom—Bob was taken from me, and I was left to travel the rest of the way alone."

The realization that we don't have control is one of the hardest illusions to relinquish. Our marriage marked the beginning of a joint journey; we struggle to accept that destiny has intervened.

It may help to think of our spouse's death as symbolic of having reached a destination—the final point that we are still approaching. He has made it all the way there—we continue along the path.

AFFIRMATION: Each of us has our own path to travel.

OTHER MEN

She found someone new before the body was even cold.
—MEAN-SPIRITED GOSSIP

It is rare for women to fall in love quickly following the loss of their husband. But it happens—and it happens for lots of understandable reasons.

We are terribly lonely, seeking solace in the arms of another. We are scared, grasping for the security of having someone to care for us. We are depressed and want to escape our pain.

Although there are certainly exceptions to the rule, most romances that ignite during bereavement are short-lived and premature, usually rebound attempts at ameliorating our sadness rather than bonds based on genuine affections and love. If, however, you find yourself in this situation, be compassionate. Don't heap judgment or criticism upon yourself. This is merely another perfectly human way to cope.

AFFIRMATION: I will go easy on myself.

It might be more helpful if people would talk about death and dying as an intrinsic part of life just as they do not hesitate to mention when someone is having a baby.

—ELISABETH KÜBLER-ROSS

In our culture birth is celebrated, death is mourned. In some East Indian cultures it is reversed: Birth is considered the beginning of a long, hard struggle, whereas death is perceived as a triumphant culmination—cause for communal joy.

At a hospital in Toledo, Ohio, every time a baby is born, Brahms's Lullaby is played over the loudspeaker system. For those few moments everyone is reminded of the sanctity of birth.

We would do well to dramatically, symbolically acknowledge the universality of death as well, perhaps with an appropriate piece of music or a moment of silent prayer publicly announcing the moment of this profound life passage.

AFFIRMATION: Death is a natural part of life.

BARGAINING

Most bargains are made with God.
—ELISABETH KÜBLER-ROSS

According to Kübler-Ross, bargaining is the third stage of the grief process. First we experience denial, then anger once reality sets in, then we begin negotiating, making "deals with God" in an effort to alter a reality that's still too hard to bear.

Bargaining is something most of us have experience with, anytime we feel helpless and would do anything to change the outcome of a difficult situation. The night before my father had his first triple bypass, I vowed to quit smoking if his surgery was successful. Three months after her husband's death Rita found herself promising God that she'd never again fight with George if she could just have him back, knowing full well it would take a full-blown miracle.

But then, bargaining isn't rational. It's simply our mind's and heart's way of working through our wishes until we are ready to accept the truth.

AFFIRMATION: I accept the fact that he's gone.

Bargaining is the term for the stage of grieving in which we offer "deals to God" in exchange for having our beloved back. Although it may seem ridiculous and futile (after all, we know better than to expect results!), the actual process is a necessary way of moving from rage to acceptance.

Here's your chance to put it in words. In the following space write a letter to your love telling him what bargains you've offered up for his return. You might use these words:

My Dearest_____,

   If I could have you back, I'd . . .

*In desperate hope I go and search for her in all the
corners of my room.*

—RABINDRANATH TAGORE

The desperate search to recover our beloved occurs during
the bargaining stage of grieving. We know he's gone, yet we
walk upstairs, fantasizing we'll see him shaving in the bathroom. In the morning, before we're fully conscious, we may
wake with the momentary belief that we will find him, safe
and warm, lying beside us. One widow, Debra, jumped out
of a taxicab in the middle of a snowstorm, certain she saw
her husband, Thomas, who had been dead three years, walking down the street. She says, "The mind plays amazing
tricks. I could have sworn it was Tom, I guess because I so
badly wanted it to be."

The "search" is yet another coping mechanism, a futile
attempt to deny the undeniable that helps us make the transition from bargaining to acceptance, from looking for our
mate to living with his absence.

AFFIRMATION: Where are you?

Even those of us who reject religion may speculate about the possibility of an afterlife. Is there a heaven or a hell? What's happened to our dearly departed? Is he resting comfortably? Floating amid the clouds? Reunited with friends and relatives who reside in the afterworld?

In the following space write a letter to your love asking for details. Express all your questions, no matter how silly or mystical they seem. Begin with these words:

My Dearest_____,

Where are you and what are you doing?

RESTIMULATION

Every loss recapitulates earlier losses.
                                    —MARY CATHERINE BATESON

Many psychologists, philosophers, and theologians believe that one of the reasons grief is so wrenching is that we are mourning not only our present loss but all the losses we've accumulated over time.

It's a staggering proposition. And it makes sense. Our mate's death may reactivate all sorts of painful loss and separation—the death of a parent, the breakup of a marriage or romance. Any grievous disappointment may resurface as we let our defenses down and allow ourselves to feel our pain.

This is one of those good-news/bad-news phenomena. Our mourning is intensified by reliving layers of losses. But in the process we have the opportunity of a lifetime to heal.

AFFIRMATION: I welcome the chance to complete unfinished business.

Sometimes I wish that I his pillow were,
So I might steale a kiss.

—RICHARD BARNFIELD

Kissing. Of the widows I interviewed for this book, not one mentioned missing it, although I suspect it's one of the sweetest and most intangible losses we incur.

"Good morning" kisses still damp with sleep; coming through the front door "How was your day, dear?" kisses; passionate kisses in the heat of lovemaking that said more than all the words in the English language and then some.

We yearn for them all. They represented comfort, security, lust, and above all the love that sometimes could only be spoken through the meeting of two lips, matched perfectly, missed terribly.

AFFIRMATION: One last kiss.

HUMOR

Death is nature's way of saying, "Your table is ready."
— ROBIN WILLIAMS

It may be a while before we regain our sense of humor. Although it may seem sacrilegious to joke about death, just the opposite is true. The capacity to lighten up occasionally, to see the absurdity, to laugh even in the worst moments, is a statement of healing and hope. Laughter also is a coping mechanism, a way of accepting the unacceptable by putting it in humorous perspective.

This quote made me laugh. And it makes death a little less scary. A little more ordinary. A little easier to accept.

AFFIRMATION: I can laugh about it too.

I don't understand why we pray to God. Why don't we just pray to each other?

—ZOE STERN

There is power and comfort in turning to a higher power, but there is equal power in turning to one another for solace and sanctuary.

Healing is enhanced by our capacity to be receptive to empathy, human touch, and other efforts to connect on the part of our loved ones. Praying to one another—and, more importantly, *with* one another—has mystical power beyond what we may rationally comprehend.

Which is why attending church, temple, or other communal spiritual gatherings can ease our isolation and bolster our faith.

This is not for everybody. For some widows public worship is far too vulnerable. For others there is power in sheer numbers, power in witnessing other people's burdens, power in a chorus of voices raised in song and prayer and love.

AFFIRMATION: My community is here to support me.

MONTH SEVEN   **DAY FOURTEEN**

Won't you come into the garden? My roses would like to see you.

—RICHARD B. SHERIDAN

If you indulge in one area, make it flowers. A bouquet of fresh tulips, delicate roses, or breathtaking irises is one sure way to reconnect with life when death weighs heavily on our mind.

Planting a garden also yields plentiful rewards. We put on our oldest, most comfortable dungarees, dig in the dirt, participate in creation, sow seeds for the future.

Besides, gardening is a wonderful way to pass time in solitude, to listen to ourselves without pressure to converse, without feeling as if we *ought* to be doing something productive, without feeling as if we *ought* to be anywhere else.

And so we water our tomatoes, talk—and listen—to our roses, plant our perennials, and perhaps shed a few tears in the privacy of our garden, reconnecting to life, to hope, to nature in all her majesty.

AFFIRMATION: I will surround myself with nature's bounty.

I struggled recently because I got Jim's autopsy report. I was devastated; almost every bone in his body had been broken.

—GEORGANN FULLER

Another hard decision that falls into the "How much reality can I bear?" category.

We may or may not have chosen to see our beloved's body in the casket, we may or may not have chosen to read the autopsy report—both examples of tough "reality checks" that can be empowering acts of healing or unnecessarily painful experiences.

Some widows say that witnessing his deceased body was a hard, yet helpful way of coming to terms with the finality of their spouse's death. Others would rather avoid carrying around these images, preferring to remember him alive and well.

Likewise some widows say that a thorough reading of the autopsy report served to resolve unanswered questions, bringing them one step closer to acceptance. For others the autopsy report is another harsh blow, confirming our worst fears, especially when it contains graphic and gruesome details, as in the case of violent death.

Like so many aspects of bereavement, these are deeply personal decisions. Only you can know how much you care to know.

AFFIRMATION: I'll investigate only that information that will help me heal.

LOOKING GOOD

One of the paramount reasons for staying attractive is so you can have somebody to go to bed with.
                                        —Helen Gurley Brown

Please! After so many years of reading women's magazines we've been brainwashed into thinking the point of keeping ourselves fit and attractive is to engage the attentions of a man.

If we buy into this, then right now we may as well let ourselves go to hell; we've lost our lover, our sex life is nonexistent, and we may not be in the market for another, in which case why bother looking good?

Here are three good reasons:

- Pride—looking good is a matter of self-respect. Being widowed is *not* an excuse for looking dowdy.
- Health and well-being—nutrition, exercise, and even a flattering wardrobe all contribute to our overall sense of well-being.
- Staying attractive makes *us* feel good—and there's no better reason than that!

AFFIRMATION: I look good for myself first and foremost.

*He has her eyes. I now see the lineage even more clearly
than before.*

—JONATHAN LAZEAR

In his lovely memoir *Remembrances of Mother* Jonathan Lazear
is speaking of the comfort in seeing his son, Ross's, resem-
blance to his late mother.

As widows we, too, take comfort in the ways our children
look like, sound like, and act like their father in so many
different ways. Noticing the similarities is both painful and
powerfully healing. Our son's shock of carrot-red curls
makes us ache to run our hand through our husband's hair.
Our daughter's dry sense of humor, perfect pitch, and canny
ability to predict a thunderstorm's approach is so evocative
of her father that it sends shivers down our spine.

Our children—the bearers of his lineage, his proud legacy
—are the ultimate evidence of our loss and of our love. We
look at them and say:

AFFIRMATION: In you your father lives on.

I'm afraid to die and leave my kids orphaned.
—LOTS OF YOUNGER WIDOWS

If we're widowed young, we may feel extremely terrified of leaving our children orphaned if, God forbid, something happens to us. Before, the thought of dying while our children were growing up was horrifying, but at least we felt secure that their other parent would be there for them. Now it's all on our shoulders; we feel extremely vulnerable just thinking about the possibility of leaving them parentless.

Although the likelihood of this tragedy is slight, we can actively prepare for the contingency by appointing legal guardians for our children. Most people choose a close family member; dear friends are also an option.

Again, you will, hopefully, live to see your children enter adulthood. But getting this piece of legal and emotional business in place will help put your mind at rest.

AFFIRMATION: I will put my own affairs in order.

I am so very tired sometimes of trying. I'm trying all the time.

—Ann, *Exposure*

These words bring tears to my eyes because they're so, so true. Surviving takes an incredible amount of energy; we're tired of trying to handle so much responsibility, tired of trying to be strong and brave, tired of trying to be optimistic, tired of trying to make ourselves get out in the world, make friends, make plans, make sense out of what's happened, tired of trying to help our children heal, tired of trying graciously to accept other people's condolences, tired of trying to get over our pain so that we can get on with our lives.

So what do we do when we're tired? We give ourselves a break. We rest, let down, and give ourselves permission to stop trying for a while. It's hard to stop; it feels like giving up. In fact it's a way of giving ourselves the greatest gift of all when we can say:

AFFIRMATION: I don't have to try. I just have to be.

Surround yourself with things that are alive.
— MELBA COLGROVE, HAROLD BLOOMFIELD,
AND PETER MCWILLIAMS

The authors of *How to Survive the Loss of a Love* recommend that in addition to family and friends, it's helpful and healing to invite plants, kittens, puppies, goldfish, even a bowl of fresh fruit to remind you that the universe is growing, thriving, blossoming despite our loss.

One widow, Carrie, planted a rosebush in her backyard as a symbol of her love and an affirmation of life. Another widow, Helen, buys herself a bouquet of lilies once a week as an antidote to her loss.

Things that are alive remind us that life is worth living. Planting tomatoes, playing with grandchildren, visiting the newborn nursery at the hospital—all balance our preoccupation with death and renew our faith and optimism.

AFFIRMATION: The universe is alive and well.

Many people have told us, "I am not sure if I am grieving his absence now or my absence then."
—STEPHEN LEVINE

Our mate's death makes us intensely aware of the times when we weren't "there" for him, when we were emotionally inaccessible, distracted, or just too busy to pay attention.

We grieve the lost opportunities and feel helplessly, hopelessly incapable of recovering them. In death there are no second chances, which is terribly difficult to accept. This is where guilt and grief intersect; the more we beat ourselves up for the ways we could have been more loving, the worse we feel.

There is a way out of this seemingly black hole. We forgive ourselves by saying:

AFFIRMATION: I did the best with what I had at the time.

PITY

Pity has a quality of considerable need about it.
> —STEPHEN LEVINE

Which is one of the reasons it doesn't feel particularly good when offered.

Whereas sympathy comes from a genuine desire to empathize, pity seems to require that the other person be helped to get over his or her pain. "I feel for you" means "I care about how you are feeling." In contrast "I feel sorry for you" translates into "Oh, you poor thing, I feel so terrible about your tragedy."

The last thing we need right now is to take care of anyone else's feelings. It's not fair and, while it's not malicious, it's a selfish and disrespectful way of responding.

When we encounter pity, we can counteract it by saying:

AFFIRMATION: Thank you very much, but your pity is wasted on me.

Six out of ten American widows live below the official poverty line.

—NATIONAL BUREAU OF STATISTICS

This staggering statistic is a serious message to all women. Whether we're single, married, widowed, or divorced, it ought to galvanize us into action in three important ways: First, it can motivate us to be as self-reliant as possible so that we're never again in the position of being impoverished as a result of economic dependence. Second, it reminds us to raise our daughters and granddaughters to be educated and fully capable of making a reasonable living. Finally, it charges us to be politically active—to fight for women's rights to equal opportunity in the workforce so that someday this statistic will be an artifact we've had a hand in making obsolete. So that no widow will ever again have to face poverty as part of her loss.

AFFIRMATION: May the future be brighter and more secure for all women everywhere.

Are You Aware of All Your Assets?

Financial assets, that is. Locating records of all checking accounts, savings accounts, stocks, bonds, and other investments will help you feel that much more secure. If you and your husband made joint financial decisions, you may already be privy to exactly what you have. If not, it's important to find out so that you can make wise and informed decisions.

My favorite thing is to go where I've never been.
                                                    —DIANE ARBUS

Widowhood involves so many opportunities to experiment in ways we may never have before, to go places previously unexplored.

Regardless of how much our mate encouraged us to seek adventure and fulfill our dreams, most marriages involve certain parameters that limit our scope. We may have always fantasized about taking up scuba diving, but our husband's disinterest kept us from signing up for classes. Perhaps our love for dancing was tabled due to our mate's two left feet. Before we were married, we may have loved to peruse bookstores, but our mutual lifestyle simply didn't lend itself to this—now we can browse to our heart's content.

Being widowed—for all its loss—also presents the freedom to make fresh discoveries, develop unexplored parts of ourselves, venture into unknown territory sure to make us feel more alive.

AFFIRMATION: I've always wanted to . . .

Don't hate, it's too big a burden to bear.
—MARTIN LUTHER KING, JR.

We may be so consumed with rage, it temporarily turns to hatred. We may hate the doctors who, for all their medical breakthroughs, still couldn't save our mate. We may hate our friends who, despite their condolences, remain happily coupled. We may hate innocent phone callers who ask for our husband. We may hate religious leaders whose efforts at compassion leave us cold, we may even hate God for his/her hand in this cruel twist of fate.

In short we may hate anyone and everyone for a while, including ourselves, until our rage is spent, until the sadness beneath our anger surfaces. Until we are ready to say:

AFFIRMATION: My hatred has been healed.

O God, full of compassion, dwelling on high, grant
perfect rest under the wings of thy presence.
                    —JEWISH MEMORIAL PRAYER

In his book *Live and Learn and Pass It On,* H. Jackson Browne,
Jr, includes, "I've learned that everyone can use a prayer."

This one seems right. Whether or not we embrace the
concept of God or a higher being, we surely ask that our
beloved be granted perfect rest, perfect peace, perfect sanctuary under the wings of whatever holy presence exists in the
universe.

If prayer is a regular part of your life, it may be an especially powerful healing agent right now. If prayer isn't comfortable or right for you, consider the spiritual sages who
said, "All prayer is longing." In whatever feels right, express your longing, your gratitude, your desire to be reunited with your mate.

AFFIRMATION: I am filled with longing.

No person is your friend who demands your silence.
—ALICE WALKER

Amen! If any of your friends try to silence you by changing the subject, making you feel as if your need to talk about your grief is excessive, walk away! Not because they're mean or malicious but because your need to process your pain takes precedence over their discomfort.

It's essential to allow yourself to talk as much as you want; healing is hastened by reminiscing about your husband, processing the last days of his life, the funeral, and any other details surrounding his death. For now choose only to spend time with people who are supportive and understanding, who can lovingly listen as long as you need to talk.

But even the best friends have limitations. Talking to a minister or rabbi, professional therapist or grief counselor, can also be an alternative sounding board and source of comfort.

AFFIRMATION: There's still so much to say.

*This pure grief reveals to me the degree of fulfillment
that Phil and I came to together.*

        —DR. ALLA RENEE BOZARTH

Which is another way of saying that the degree of our loss is
in direct proportion to the depth of our love.

If we hadn't given ourselves heart, body, and soul, we
wouldn't be suffering nearly so much. If we hadn't loved so
thoroughly, so selflessly, we wouldn't feel so lost. If we
hadn't been so compatible, we wouldn't feel so estranged. If
we hadn't so completely invested ourselves in the vision of
our shared future, tomorrow wouldn't seem so bleak.

At times our grief makes us wish we hadn't loved so
intensely. Perhaps the pain would be easier to bear. But deep
down we know better. And we wouldn't take back an ounce
of our love. In the words of Mother Teresa:

AFFIRMATION: I have learned to "love until it hurts."

She was my protector, my comforter, my ally.
—JONATHAN LAZEAR

These adjectives, used to describe a deceased mother, could just as easily be attributed to our late spouse.

He was my protecter: the one I could depend on to take care of me, to keep me safe and warm.

He was my comforter: the one I could turn to when I needed reassurance, when I needed to hear the words "Honey, it will be all right."

He was my ally: the one person in the world I could count on as my loyal partner with whom to face the adversities in life.

It is no wonder we feel so vulnerable, at times insecure, and painfully alone. And it's no wonder we question if we will ever, ever feel quite so blessed again.

AFFIRMATION: I had so much.

*What is our moral responsibility to prolong life and
when shall we feel free to permit the angel of death to
carry out its task?*

—RABBI ZACHARY I. HELLER

If our spouse's death followed a long-drawn-out illness, we
may at some point have been confronted with the decision
about continuing life support. Hopefully our mate had made
his position known, verbally or through a living will. Knowing what he wanted, even if it wasn't what *we* wanted, left us
with a clear conscience and the confidence that we were
carrying out his wishes. If, however, we had to guess, we
may still feel anxious, guilty, or remorseful. If we chose to
prolong life, we may worry that in doing so we also pro-
longed his pain. If we chose to intervene in an effort to end
his suffering, we may be wracked with anguish that we in
some way expedited his death.

These feelings, however irrational, are real. If they play
heavily on your mind and heart, seek counseling, perhaps
from a spiritual adviser or therapist specializing in grief.
Making peace with yourself—and whatever decisions you
were called upon to make—is essential to moving on.

**AFFIRMATION: I made the wisest, most loving deci-
sion possible under the circumstances.**

ENJOYMENT

*There is no cure for birth and death save to enjoy the
interval.*

——GEORGE SANTAYANA

Even those activities that previously brought a smile to our
face may now seem a strain: dinner with friends, playing
with our grandchildren, seeing an Academy Award–winning
film, may be forced obligations we'd just as soon cancel so
that we can crawl back into bed.

Forcing ourselves to "enjoy" is a bit like stuffing down a
hot fudge sundae when we have a stomach flu; not only are
we incapable of savoring it, the experience makes us sick.
Eventually our capacity for enjoyment will return. Meanwhile here's a tip from other widows: Start by engaging in
solitary pleasures: reading, gardening, TV, or anything else
you can do on your own. Then slowly start spending time
with one dear friend, then another, until you're able to enjoy
the company of others without feeling pressured. If they
truly love you, they'll back off until you're ready to make
overtures.

AFFIRMATION: I'll take it slow.

Thus we live, forever taking leave.

—RAINER MARIA RILKE

Our awareness of impermanence has been enhanced by our loss. Now when we bid farewell to friends and acquaintances after spending time together, we realize there are no guarantees of coming back together in the morning light. We've learned that everything can—and will—be taken from us, that partings are an integral part of life, that reunions mustn't be taken for granted.

And so we say our good-byes with greater care, taking an extra moment for a hug, a warm word of encouragement, a prayer for safekeeping as our loved ones go their separate ways. We remember to say, "Be well," or "I love you," words that come from having lived through more days than we can count, wishing we had another chance to say good-bye, in just the right way, just one more time.

AFFIRMATION: Until we meet again.

Have You Arranged for Your Own Personal Credit?

You may or may not have credit in your own name. If your checking accounts and credit lines are in both your names, be sure to notify the bank and businesses of the change in your marital status. If, like many women, your credit was auxiliary or completely under the auspices of your husband's name, it's time to do whatever possible to establish financial independence.

A checking account is the best place to start. Transferring your car payments, utility bills, and department-store credit cards to your own name will help you build a positive credit history. If this feels overwhelming, it's well worth it to hire a financial adviser to guide you through this process.

We have promises to keep and miles to go before we sleep.

—ROBERT FROST

We may have made promises to our spouse prior to his death, ranging from concrete commitments, such as agreeing to get the painter to finish the bathroom, to more serious, long-ranging promises, such as the one my neighbor, Susan, made to her late ex-husband, Bruce, on his deathbed.

"It was terribly important to Bruce that our daughter, Molly, be raised in the Jewish tradition," says Susan, who faithfully fulfilled her commitment, no small feat since she herself isn't Jewish. She enrolled her daughter in Sunday school, observed the holidays, and made a beautiful bat mitzvah, at which Bruce's prayer shawl was draped around Molly by his two brothers in a poignant act of remembrance.

Some promises we can keep; others may need to be renegotiated over time. What matters is to do all we can to honor our commitments.

AFFIRMATION: I will keep—or renegotiate—the promises I've made to my mate.

We may have made promises to our dying spouse, some that we have already fulfilled and others that we still intend to fulfill. There may be still other promises that we are unwilling or unable to keep. Here's your chance to write a letter to your departed mate, letting him know what commitments you've continued to honor and explaining your reasons for those that must be renegotiated in the light of what you feel or can do today. You might begin with these words:

My Dearest_____,

   I know I promised to . . .

You can give without loving, but you cannot love without giving.

—AMY CARMICHAEL

Repeatedly I hear widows say that one of the greatest losses is not having someone to love, to give to and care for now that their mate is no longer alive.

So much of loving is not what we get but what we give. We derived such deep satisfaction from generously extending ourselves: tending to our spouse's needs by listening to his feelings; supporting the pressures of his career; feeding and nurturing him by making palatable meals, by making love, by making sure he knew we were unconditionally there for him in a million different ways.

We miss the opportunity to give. Although it will be in far different ways, we still have so much to offer the other loved ones in our lives. Our children, our friends, the other members of our family can benefit from our ongoing outpouring of love.

AFFIRMATION: I still have so much to give.

SOLITUDE

*Perhaps now and then a castaway on a lonely desert
island dreads the thought of being rescued.*
                                        —SARAH ORNE JEWETT

Others may want to rescue us from our loneliness and grief.
They may invite us to dinner, urge us to attend social gatherings, suggest trips, seminars, or other activities to distract us
from pain and speed up our healing.

But their efforts, however well intentioned, may have just
the opposite effect. We may embrace our emptiness right
now, which is different from wallowing in it. Our loneliness
is bittersweet; our pain is a powerful testament to our love
for our mate, for which escape is merely a Band-Aid, a
temporary remedy for a long-term recovery process.

Sometimes our friends' rescue efforts are welcome; other
times they feel like pressure and intrusion. At these times we
can graciously respond by saying:

AFFIRMATION: Thank you, but I need to be alone.

If we have lost our spouse, we have also lost the part of him that drove us nuts.

— STEPHANIE ERICCSON

We wouldn't opt for it, but we can still appreciate the absence of annoying habits that we no longer must deal with since our spouse's death.

Admitting to ourselves that there are things about him we *don't* miss may seem hard and heartless. "I felt like a real jerk when I realized how nice it was not having to listen to Seth grumble about money," says Nan, who admits she now indulges in occasional luxuries her late husband vetoed. Another widow, Beth, says, "Although I miss Tom every single day, I *don't* miss his piles of underwear all over the bathroom floor."

Obviously there's no trade-off here. We'd give anything to have him back—flaws and all—but since we can't, we may as well accept the ways, however trivial, that life has changed for the better.

AFFIRMATION: I don't miss . . .

MEANING

*Facing death means facing the ultimate question of the
meaning of life.*

—Elisabeth Kübler-Ross

As we grieve our mate's death, we think often about the
meaning of *his* life. We evaluate his actions and achievements, we wonder if he was happy, satisfied, and fulfilled,
we try to make sense of his death by defining the quality of
his existence.

But having faced death, we are also called upon to ponder
the meaning of our *own* lives. Being widowed is a wake-up
call; it motivates us seriously to consider who we are and
why we're here on earth.

Our experience has taught us that life is short, that we
must proceed with intention and integrity in order to be
fully alive. In this way our grief is a gift—we rededicate
ourselves to a life filled with purpose and meaning.

AFFIRMATION: Why am I here?

I'm working overtime so that I don't come unglued.
—IRIS DEMENT

Workaholism is now commonly included under the umbrella of addictive behaviors. Why? Because obsessive working can be used as a "drug" of sorts, as a way of anesthetizing our pain.

As in any potentially addictive behavior, moderation is the key; if we're running to the office as a way of running away from our grief, we need to stop and find the balance between healthy distraction and self-destructive escape.

Here's the difference: If work is satisfying *and* if it doesn't mask your feelings, then by all means put as much energy as you want into your vocation or career. If, however, you feel frantic, inordinately absorbed with work, and numbed to your sorrow, then you may have crossed the line.

Keeping busy is good. Working overtime will only postpone your grief—and your healing.

AFFIRMATION: I will find the right balance between working and resting.

*Why would I want to read a widow's memoir? What
could she possibly know about what I'm going through?*
—HELEN K.

We may bristle at suggestions that our grief is knowable, that
anyone on earth has experienced anything remotely similar,
much less have something to offer us in the way of information and support.

As Stephen Levine, author of *Healing into Life and Death*
says, "We expect our grief to be something special." And of
course it is. Even those individuals whose experiences closely
mirror our own can't get inside our skin, can't fully comprehend our unique loss. They can, however, inform our journey by sharing their own.

We can guide one another, understanding that our grief is
both ordinary and extraordinary, both singular and universal,
both something others can relate to and that which cannot be
known.

**AFFIRMATION: Others have been there before me. I
can learn from their experience.**

There are exceptions to all rules—and I am one of them.

—FORREST GUMP

This book, along with others dealing with grief and healing, is filled with suggestions based on "common experience." Most books can't help but generalize: "most widows feel . . . ," "most widows need . . . ," "most widows discover . . . ," and on and on.

Even as we say that there are no hard-and-fast rules to mourning, it's assumed that everyone fundamentally shares similar feelings, that most, if not all, widows go through a set process. It's also assumed that anyone who has lost his or her spouse can be expected to act in certain, predictable ways and can be comforted through universal acts of kindness and compassion.

And so I offer this caveat: There are exceptions to all rules, and you may be one of them. Don't allow yourself to be categorized; don't expect yourself to fit anyone's—including my own—description of widows.

Honor your individuality and *insist* on being yourself.

AFFIRMATION: I am an individual and won't be categorized.

I've lost my best friend.

—MOST WIDOWS

He was more than just our husband, lover, and father of our children. He was our very best friend—and in some ways this is the greatest loss of all.

He was our shoulder to cry on, our support system when we were confused or in need of advice, our playmate, confidant, traveling companion, the one person with whom we could sit in bed eating Chinese food and watching television without the need for any formality whatsoever.

In short we could be ourselves and know we could depend on his unconditional love and support. Even when we argued, even when we got on each other's nerves, we felt his devotion, counted on his friendship.

We have other friends—for whom we're now more grateful than ever before. But we continue to be grief-stricken that our very best friend is no longer at our side.

AFFIRMATION: Thank you for being my very best friend.

MONTH EIGHT   **DAY FIFTEEN**

Having someone wonder where you are when you don't come home at night is a very old human need.

—MARGARET MEAD

We're used to his greeting as we walk through the door, hearing his eager voice ask, "Honey, did you have a good time?" He made us know that one person in the world was consistently concerned with our well-being, glad to have us home, safe and sound.

Now we may dread coming home, staying away later than we really want to just to avoid the inevitable moment of facing the void we feel when we walk through the door. We may be afraid of the dark; there's nothing childish about it, after years and years of his comforting presence. For weeks following my divorce I was terrified of walking into my house at night; I'll always be grateful to my friend, Michael, who, upon sensing my apprehension, drove halfway across town on a snowy winter night to check for monsters lurking underneath the bed.

Asking a friend to walk in with you, leaving lights lit, the television or radio on (I know it's a waste of energy, but if it helps, do it!), and returning before dusk are all ways of easing your own fears until coming home at night gets easier to handle.

AFFIRMATION: For a while I may be afraid of the dark. I'll make it easier in any way I can.

> *She [her friend, Eleanora Duse] never said, "Cease to grieve," but she grieved with me.*
>
> —ISADORA DUNCAN

What a gift! It's an incredible blessing to have friends capable of being totally present for our pain, so filled with empathy that they can travel alongside our journey.

Most of our friends fall somewhere on the spectrum between avoiding our pain, encouraging us to "get over it," and being extraordinarily willing to be a companion in our grief. In other words even our closest, truest friends can be there some of the time but not all of the time.

That's where professional counseling comes in. Feeling our pain in the presence of someone familiar with the terrain of suffering, someone who won't hurry us through our grieving but rather will sit with us for as long as it takes helps us appreciate (and forgive our friends) while getting the support we need.

AFFIRMATION: I can turn to numerous and varied resources for support.

Being married gives one position like nothing else can.
                                                   —QUEEN VICTORIA

Sad but true. Even in this relatively liberal, nonsexist culture, where single women aren't looked upon as second-class
citizens, marriage *still* affords a degree of status that sepa-
rates the Misses from the Missuses.

As widows we feel the discrimination in a number of
different ways: when the maître d' at our favorite restaurant
is less solicitous than when we were accompanied by our
husband; when we receive less than preferential treatment—
and sometimes outright mistreatment—from everyone from
the plumber to our accountant, who used to bend over back-
ward catering to our mate; when married friends delete us
from their social calendar; when our husband's business asso-
ciates no longer afford us the same respect we automatically
inspired when we enjoyed the elevated status of "wife."

We aren't about to change such rude and retrograde atti-
tudes. But we *can* make every effort not to take these slights
personally. They can—and should—make us mad. But ultimately they're not worth getting worked up over. Instead we
can say:

AFFIRMATION: I'm still the same woman I was.

I confess to Joseph that I have a terrible secret. "I caused Mel's cancer."

—ANNE HOSANSKY

This confession revealed in a grief group was surprisingly followed by a chorus of "Me too's" and "I know what you mean, I feel exactly the same way!"

However irrational, feeling vaguely—or even directly—responsible for our husband's death is a powerfully real, typical response. As Hosansky, in her memoir, *Widow's Walk,* explains, "We argued a lot. I didn't accept him the way he was. . . . He hadn't been looking well and I told him he should get a checkup, but I didn't *push* it."

Stop! There is absolutely nothing you could have done to prevent his death, and you *certainly* didn't cause it! This is one situation in which it helps to pay attention to facts, to heed your rational judgment, to let your mind inform your heart. If you continue to feel that somehow you have blood on your hands, seek professional help to release you from this self-imposed bondage.

AFFIRMATION: It's not my fault.

We shared something so intimate, we shared his death.
—DEANNE BURKE

The moment of his death may have been one of the most intimate moments we shared throughout all the years of our marriage. Lingering resentments and unresolved conflicts melted away as we both confronted impending separation. On his deathbed he may have shared confidences, been more vulnerable, said "I love you" in ways previously unexpressed. We may have made amends to each other, cried in each other's arms, exposed the innermost recesses of our being in anticipation of death.

And that is something to be deeply grateful for. When it mattered, when it was still possible, we shared an intimacy worthy of our love.

AFFIRMATION: Till death do us part.

MUTUALITY

I am incapable of looking at baseball, the sport we both loved and watched together endlessly.

—RUTH COUGHLIN

Our shared passions are painfully empty without his participation. Together we ate hot dogs and watched every World Series, but now that we're alone, we can barely stand to hear the score. Our season tickets to the orchestra sit in their envelope on the mantel; we can't bring ourselves to work in our garden, where we spent so many peaceful afternoons together planting tomatoes.

For quite a while everything that reminds us of our mate may intensify our sorrow. In time we may be able to cheer on the Cubs without weeping, sit transfixed through Beethoven's Ninth, tend our perennials without acutely experiencing his absence. Meanwhile we can gradually pursue other, solo endeavors that aren't steeped in memories of happier days.

AFFIRMATION: Some things are best left alone. Meanwhile I will pursue new interests.

I want to be five years old again for an hour.
—ROBERT FULGHUM

There are days when it all feels like too much. Getting out of bed takes a Herculean effort; we can barely summon the energy to brush our teeth, much less pay bills, go to work, care for our children, and all the other demands that haven't diminished just because we're grieving.

In short we wish we could be five years old again. Being a grown-up, with its attendant responsibilities, is simply more than we can handle. We wish someone would take over, tell us what to do, or better yet do it for us. We wish we could curl up in our mother's lap as she softly murmurs, "Don't worry, honey. Everything will be all right."

We can't turn back time, but we *can* give ourselves permission to be "little"—by keeping demands to a minimum, by letting our loved ones care for us, and most of all by allowing ourselves to say:

AFFIRMATION: I don't always have to be a big girl.

Tears may be dried up, but the heart—never.
                                        —MARGUERITE DE VALOIS

There comes a time when tears dry up; we've wept so much, now we are surprised to find ourselves navigating through entire days, even weeks, without so much as our eyes welling up at the thought of him.

Which doesn't mean our heart has hardened or our love has diminished. Our hearts continue to overflow with affection: we can remain deeply in love without dissolving into a pile of tears.

As we become more adjusted to our circumstances, more accustomed to coping without him, we become stronger and less prone to emotional outbursts. And then, without notice, the tears return as we're flooded with memories of how much we've loved and lost.

AFFIRMATION: I'm having a good cry.

I'm doing the best I can.

—COELEEN KIEBERT

This generic quotation may be the most useful of all. We tend to be perfectionistic, to expect too much of ourselves, even when it comes to grief. We lay any number of *shoulds* on ourselves: *I* should *be coping better by now. I* should *pick myself up and start having a social life. I* should *be happier and more hopeful. I* should *be more immersed in sorrow. . . .*

The list goes on and on. And it's all incorrect, expect for this one *should:* I *should* stop criticizing myself and start congratulating myself for doing the best I can under very difficult circumstances.

Begin this in the following space by listing at least three ways in which you're doing the best you can:

AFFIRMATION:

1. _____

2. _____

3. _____

His last word was, "Please. . . ."

—KARA N.

We can torture ourselves imagining he was trying to say, "Please, help me," "Please, make the pain go away," "Please, save me," or any number of desperate pleas he may have been trying to express as he fought the pull of death.

Or we can finish his sentence in another way—for example "Please, don't worry about me," or "Please take good care of yourself. I love you."

In the intensive care unit following my father's cardiac bypass surgery, at one point in his morphine haze he blurted out, "I think I'm . . ." My mother, sister, and I were sure he was trying to say, "I think I'm dying." As he later informed us, he'd been dreaming he was on a luxurious cruise; he was trying to say, "I think I'm supposed to be at the midnight buffet."

So much for second-guessing our beloved's last words. We can either fill them in or live with the mystery. I recommend the latter.

AFFIRMATION: I won't let my imagination run wild.

There are things left unsaid. In the days leading up to death we tried to put all our final thoughts into words, to express everything in our minds and in our hearts before time ran out.

Depending on the circumstances of death—whether he was lucid, how quickly he failed, our own state of mind—we may or may not have said everything we needed to. Even if we tried, in retrospect there is more to say. Now's our chance. In the following space tell him all the things you didn't have a chance to before he was gone. You may repeat this exercise every few months as new things come to mind.

My Dearest_____,

Have I told you that . . .

Before Papa's funeral, the rabbi read me a book called
The Fall of Freddie the Leaf. *I highly recommend it.*
                                        —ZOE STERN

I'll go one step farther than my daughter and say I highly
recommend this lovely and profound little book for grown-
ups as well as for children.

It's the story of a leaf's movement through the seasons
and its natural death as it completes the cycle, drifting slowly
from the branches above. Here are my favorite words from
this metaphorical fairy tale:

> "Will we all die?" Freddie asked.
>
> "Yes," Daniel answered. "Everything dies. No mat-
> ter how big or small, how weak or strong. We first do
> our job. We experience the sun and the moon, the
> wind and the rain. We learn to dance and to laugh.
> Then we die."

Like Freddie the Leaf's, our birth is a radiant blossoming,
and our death a gentle descent to the earth, fulfilling destiny
in reunion with the eternal.

AFFIRMATION: We are all subject to nature's cycles.

We talk too much: we should talk less and draw more.
                                        —JOHANN WOLFGANG VON GOETHE

We needn't be Goethe to sharpen our pencil, take out our sketchbook, slip on our beret (it always helps to dress the part!), and express our feelings through a medium other than language.

We can only talk so much about our loss; at times we're at a loss for words or we're simply tired of trying to express ourselves with language that falls so short of saying what's in our heart. Then it's time to sing or dance or drum or sculpt —any creative pursuit that expresses the depth of our grief.

But don't feel pressured to suddenly buy an easel or sign up for violin lessons. Active appreciation of art and music can also help spirits soar. An afternoon spent listening to our favorite music-to-cry-by or strolling through an art gallery puts us in touch with universal pain and joy—for which at times there simply are no words.

AFFIRMATION: Creativity is a powerful healing agent.

Be brave enough to accept the help of others.
    —HAROLD BLOOMFIELD AND PETER MCWILLIAMS

In times of crisis it takes courage to swallow our pride. Friends offer help, but we don't want to be a burden. We shudder at the thought of pity, we find ourselves in the uncomfortable position of needing support but not knowing how to ask.

The best way is to simply say, "Please help me." Not only is it necessary—both practically and emotionally—but it's a way of allowing our loved ones to lend a hand. If it's hard for you to accept help, try mentally reversing the situation. If someone you loved was in need, wouldn't you do anything and everything you could to lighten his or her load?

AFFIRMATION: I'll be as good to myself as I am to others.

I'm scared, and I think that's healthy.

—JANE FONDA

There's plenty to be scared of right now, and all of it is a legitimate, natural response to widowhood.

Here's a partial list of fears most widows grapple with: Fear of being alone. Fear of not having enough money. Fear of being forgotten by friends. Fear of getting through the night. Fear of making it through each day without collapsing in a heap.

Feeling and expressing our fears is healthy, as long as we don't obsess and become paralyzed by them. Instead we can respond to fear as a call to action. Begin with the following exercise: List your three worst fears. Next to each, complete this sentence: "I will reduce my fear by . . ."

AFFIRMATION:

    1. _____

    2. _____

    3. _____

Being widowed may have intensified our fears—
of our own death, abandonment, poverty, natural disasters, and just about anything else you
can think of.

On top of which the person we're accustomed
to turning to for comfort and reassurance is
gone. But we can still tell him what's on our
mind. In the following space write a letter to your
love expressing all your fears, using the words:

My Dearest_____,

   I'm so afraid of . . .

Grief is so selfish.

—MARY ELIZABETH BRADDON

Wrong! Grief may be self-absorbing, self-enriching, even self-destructive at times, but it is *never* selfish to go deeply into our pain, no matter how much time and energy it takes away from attending to the others in our life.

Anyone who tells you differently has his or her own selfish agenda; such people are so used to your undivided attention, they resent your necessary focus on yourself.

And it *is* necessary. If we ignore our grief, we become an empty shell, emotionally and spiritually bereft, incapable of giving to anyone. On the contrary, true mourning is selfless; we temporarily put aside distractions, amusements, even fulfilling endeavors in order to do the hard work of grieving, for which we should be encouraged and applauded.

AFFIRMATION: I am proud of myself for facing my grief.

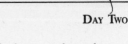

*Can you see us all and do you think we are doing the
right things?*

—JILL TRUMAN

Regardless of our religious orientation, most widows wonder
where our beloved has gone. Is he resting on celestial pillows? Is he watching from somewhere far away, and if so,
could he please give us a sign that he's at peace?

And if it's not asking too much, could he please reassure
us that he approves of how we're handling everything in his
absence? It still matters. It would be nice to know that he
appreciated how meaningful the funeral was, how courageous we were, how many people showed up to honor his
memory. Is he comfortable with how we're helping the children grieve? Not to mention the fact that we've changed the
lightbulbs, balanced the checkbook, and remembered his
mother's birthday when we had a million other things on our
mind.

We can look for signs. We can ask, through prayer, meditation, or simply straight out. But ultimately we have to
learn to say to ourselves:

AFFIRMATION: I am doing a great job!

And in the silence of this place where your body was but a mere six feet from mine, I felt the safety of your embrace.

—STEPHANIE ERICCSON

We visit his resting-place for many different reasons. We want to tell him the millions of things we've been thinking and doing and wondering about since he's been gone: The painters finally finished the bathroom, our oldest daughter got an A on her exam, one of our favorite movies was on HBO last night. We bare our soul, break down, and share our deepest emotion with the one we love best. We go to shower his grave with flowers, to meditate on his spirit, and to continue to say our good-byes.

And we go simply to be with him. To be close. To feel safe. To wrap our arms around him in the only way that remains. These are peaceful moments, when we listen to the still voice within and silently speak our love, sometimes with tears, sometimes with laughter, always knowing that here we can return.

AFFIRMATION: I am with you in spirit.

I have discovered . . . that anger is the only analgesic guaranteed to work every time.

—JOAN GOULD

At times our anger is the only way to ward off pain. And we have plenty to be angry about: the permanent loss of our lifelong companion; the plans, present and future, that have been wiped out in an instant; the numerous responsibilities, obligations, and demands that have increased as we've struggled to rebuild our lives.

Anger is productive so long as it's not turned inward, in self-destructive behavior that's hurtful or damaging. In fact it's a useful anesthetic, a way of numbing our sorrow until we're strong enough to feel it full force. Underneath the anger is sadness. Allow yourself to release it—slowly, carefully—when you're ready for the floodgates to open.

AFFIRMATION: I needn't be frightened of my anger.

Life without idealism is empty indeed. We just have hope or starve to death.

—PEARL S. BUCK

Ultimately we are left with a choice: either to become embittered or to find a way of restoring optimism and hope.

Recovering hope takes time. "It's taken nearly two years for me to believe that the world is a safe and benign place," says Rita, whose husband, Nick, waged a five-year battle against liver cancer. "I've only recently looked forward to anything," shares Helen, who admits that for almost six months after becoming widowed she felt hopeless, as if life were a daily drudge she could barely get through. "But it's starting to lift," she says. "I realized just the other day that I was excited about going on vacation this winter. I even went out and bought myself a new wardrobe for the trip."

Notice the little ways hope and optimism return. Every positive thought or action is a step in the right direction.

AFFIRMATION: I feel hopeful and optimistic about:

_____

_____

_____

> *Smiles, tears, of all my life!——and, if God choose,*
> *I shall but love thee better after death.*
> —ELIZABETH BARRETT BROWNING

We may feel more loving in the wake of our beloved's death. And for good reason: Freed of daily demands—bills to pay, joint responsibilities, aggravating idiosyncrasies—we find it easier to love and embrace him. Most widows discover a greater capacity for forgiveness through death; the little things that bug us, as well as more serious conflicts, are put in perspective, making reconciliation possible.

And mostly, in missing him we become acutely aware of how wonderful he was. Even as we acknowledge the hard times, our appreciation is enhanced. We may even fantasize a wonderful reunion, in which we are free to show him just how much we loved—and continue to love—him, especially now that he's gone.

AFFIRMATION: My fantasy reunion would be like . . .

*Take my word for it, the saddest thing under the sky is a
soul incapable of sadness.*
—COMTESSE CATHERINE DE GASPARIN

The capacity to experience profound sorrow cracks open our
heart, making us more compassionate, more humane, more
loving human beings. Having dived into the pool of anguish,
we emerge stronger for the experience. We learn that there
is nothing to be afraid of. And we gain confidence that we
will emerge on the other side.

Ultimately our sadness is a tribute to the intensity of our
love; if we didn't care so deeply, our sorrow wouldn't be
nearly so devastating. Having touched the deepest, darkest
reservoirs of sorrow, we are that much more capable of both
pain and joy.

**AFFIRMATION: I have the courage to immerse myself
in sorrow.**

SELF-DESTRUCTIVENESS

> *For almost a year after you died, I stumbled, I stubbed my toes, I closed fingers in drawers, knocked my head.*
> —ANN, *Exposure*

"As if to break through the terrible numbness, I was always calling myself back into my body, reminding myself that yes I was still here," says Ann, the main character in the novel *Exposure*, talking about her almost obsessive desire for physical pain following her father's death.

Many of us may have experienced a similar compulsion—or at least fantasy—in response to losing our spouse. The desire to feel physical pain makes sense; we're desperate to feel *anything*, to shatter our numbness, to break through paralyzing depression into violent rage, to test the limits of our physical endurance. And there's another drive—to cause ourselves physical harm as a way of connecting to our beloved, to feel some degree of the suffering he may have experienced prior to death.

There is nothing sick or wrong about manifesting our loss this way so long as we don't cause ourselves harm. If, however, you are consistently hurting yourself, seek care from a professional who can help you find other ways of making sure you're here and alive.

AFFIRMATION: I won't hurt myself anymore.

*Woman must not depend upon the protection of man,
but must be taught to protect herself.*

—SUSAN B. ANTHONY

Most of us grew up believing we could depend on the protection of men. Now as widows we must learn how to stay safe by protecting ourselves, whether it's learning how to change a flat tire, installing a home security system, or creating a support network of friends we can call upon in an emergency.

Paula carries Mace in her purse. She says, "I doubt I'll ever use it, but it makes me feel better when I'm walking from the garage to the house." "I took up karate," says Georgia, "and it's done wonders for my confidence." "I'm thinking of renting out the basement to a college student just to have another adult around," says Betsy, adding, "it would help to know there's someone else here, especially at night."

Learning to take care of ourselves is one of the challenges we face. Do anything—and everything—you can to feel safe.

AFFIRMATION: I am learning to keep myself safe and secure.

Have You Applied for Survivor's Benefits?

Here is another financial matter best attended to as soon as possible. You may be entitled to Social Security payments, pension plans, veteran's benefits, and any other compensation resulting from death.

If you're not sure how to proceed, contact the following resource:

AARP Widowed Person's Service
1909 K Street, N.W.
Washington, DC 20049

Loneliness is the most terrible poverty.

—MOTHER TERESA

"It's the loneliness that's so horrible," says Jane, my eighty-year-old mother-in-law, who, seven years after the death of her husband, Lester, still struggles to fill the void. "Sometimes I can't stand the silence," she says. "I try to make myself be social so that I won't end up alone, staring at the television."

It takes effort. Some widows find they can rely on old, trusted friends for companionship; others force themselves to be more assertive, spending more time with children or grandchildren, seeking out the company of other widows, joining clubs, taking classes, or attending singles events at synagogue or church.

The first step is the hardest, and it's compounded by our fear that now, in the midst of grieving, we're not very good company. But the more we take the initiative, the more others will reciprocate. Even if it's just a matter of filling time, sometimes it's just nice to know that we're not all alone.

AFFIRMATION: It is up to me to seek companionship.

CHANGE

Change is an easy panacea. It takes character to stay in one place and be happy there.

—ELIZABETH CLARK DUNN

We may be tempted to make quick changes as a way of anesthetizing our pain: a new home, different job, even romantic involvement. All can be dangerous detours that temporarily distract us from our grief.

For now it may be better, at least for a while, to keep changes to a minimum. Even if we eventually decide to relocate, the time we spend in our home, among our memories and shared belongings, keeps us rooted in the reality of our loss. Similarly, by resisting the urge to alter our vocation or throw ourselves into a new relationship, we are forced to find happiness without trying to escape.

A time will come when change is the healthiest option—when it's motivated by inspiration, not desperation. When it's about moving on rather than running away.

AFFIRMATION: I will remain rooted in reality.

Your pain is the breaking of the shell that encloses your understanding.

—KAHLIL GIBRAN

It is true. One reason why pain feels so shattering is because it involves a break: the tear in our heart that's so badly in need of mending. Our fractured lives in the midst of disrepair. But mostly we've experienced a break in the shell protecting our trust. Now we are open to the pain of understanding, no longer able to run away from the reality of his death. Our outer covering is removed; as it sinks in that he is gone forever, our pain is intensified.

We are left open and exposed. But the break is also a breakthrough. Beyond our pain is the possibility of rebirth, which only occurs when we are ready to burst through the shell.

AFFIRMATION: My heart is cracking open.

When loving hearts are separated, not the one which is exhaled to heaven but the survivor it is which tastes the sting of death.

—DUCHESSE DE PRASLIN

Funerals are for the living—it is the bereaved who most need comforting, which is why it's so important to give ourselves time to grieve and heal.

Most widows say it takes nearly a year to recover from the death of a loved one. Although we never completely stop missing him, the first year is especially emotionally wrought; our loss is fresh, and we need to surround ourselves with supportive friends who understand what we're going through.

We may even feel impatient with condolences directed toward our mate: "Poor Bob, he suffered so." But in the final analysis we are the ones who are suffering. It's up to us to pick up our lives and go on, despite our ever-present pain.

AFFIRMATION: I am a survivor.

I don't want to leave here because you are everywhere in this place.

—JILL TRUMAN

The decision to change residences, to sell your home or move to another location, may be fraught with indecision. Staying put can seem like stagnation; our home is filled with ghosts, reminders everywhere of our life together. Leaving, on the other hand, may be traumatic. Sorting through belongings, deciding what to keep and what to discard, is an overwhelming task. And moving on feels like another step toward saying good-bye to our old life; rationally or irrationally it seems like a form of disloyalty to the deceased.

But there is also excitement in beginning anew. Hanging up curtains, arranging furniture, creating a new environment practically and symbolically represent a new start. You needn't leave him behind. Be sure to bring a few mementos of your marriage, even if you tuck them in a drawer. Your favorite photograph of the two of you, on your nightstand or displayed on the mantel, helps bridge the transition from the past to the present.

AFFIRMATION: I will relocate if and when I'm ready.

When I met my husband I was eighteen and I remember thinking: "When I have gray hair, this is the man I want to be sitting with on the porch, watching our grandchildren play."

—COKIE ROBERTS

There was much still ahead; death has abbreviated our hopes and plans and dreams.

This, too, must be grieved. We haven't just lost our partner, we've also lost all the wonderful things we were going to do together. Our destinies were linked; he was part and parcel of our blueprint for the future.

And so we must create a new vision—one that sadly doesn't include his presence. In time new hopes and dreams will unfold as we build our future along entirely new lines.

Meanwhile the day will come when we will sit on our porch, watching our grandchildren play, knowing that somewhere he is taking it all in, just as we had always known it would be.

AFFIRMATION: I grieve the loss of my fantasies as I prepare to face the future.

People come and go in life, but they never leave your dreams.

—PATRICIA HAMPL

"I dreamed he was slowly walking toward me, but when I reached out my hand, he disintegrated into thin air," says Lynn, a widow of six months, who experiences recurring dreams in which she momentarily encounters her late husband, Matthew. "Each time, I try to get him to stay, but he can't," says Lynn, "and I wake up feeling frustrated all over again."

Another woman, Betsy, whose husband, Steven, died in a plane crash, has nightmares of a blazing fire, its flames out of control. She tries to rescue Steve, but can't get close enough to save his life. In contrast Paula, recently widowed, describes this wonderfully comforting dream: "I was walking in a meadow and saw Randy sitting on a rock," says Paula. "He looked right at me, smiled, and said, 'Everything's perfect.' I woke up and for the first time since he died, I knew in my heart that everything would be fine."

Dreams are yet another way in which we continue to bid farewell to our mate. Some are frightening, some are deeply reassuring, but in either case most widows are grateful to see him one more time, if only in our dreams.

AFFIRMATION: I'm dreaming about you.

Sooner or later we discover that we only rent our happiness.

—JOAN GOULD

First, as mothers we learned this lesson: that we are our children's temporary guardians, that sooner or later it is our task to let them go.

So, too, our beloved was only ours for whatever time he had on this earth. How fortunate we were to have held him in our arms; now we must graciously release him, grateful for the hours, days, and years spent together.

It's natural to cling to our happiness; the pangs of separation are intense, sometimes unbearable. But everything precious is fleeting; the rose blooms and fades, the snowflake dissolves within instants of meeting the ground. All that we love, all that we treasure, is ours to savor in the moment, for that is all we have.

AFFIRMATION: I'm glad for every day I had you in my life.

Because he died before I was able to reconcile with him,
I felt an enormous amount of guilt and sorrow.
                                          —LINDA LEONARD

Our sorrow becomes compounded if we are left with unfinished business; unresolved conflicts, estrangement, or arguments haunt us, seemingly impossible to reconcile now that it's too late.

But it isn't really too late. Guilt only serves as a useful reminder that it's time to make amends. Death is always inopportune, but sometimes its timing is especially difficult. We wish we could apologize for the ways in which we caused hurt. We'd give anything to heal the rifts, to say, "I'm sorry. Our love is more important than who is right."

So say it now. Make amends in whatever way feels right: out loud, to him; on paper, in the form of a letter; in your prayers, asking forgiveness.

Then forgive yourself.

AFFIRMATION: I'm sorry.

You can't be brave if you've only had wonderful things happen to you.

—MARY TYLER MOORE

I know, you're tired of hearing how suffering builds character; but of course you know it's true.

You've had to be brave, and it's taught you something important—that in the toughest of times you have the inner resilience to take what comes with the courage of a warrior. You've had to be brave for him in the throes of his suffering, carrying out arrangements with grace and dignity when all you wanted was to curl up in a corner and cry.

And now you carry on, even on those days when your courage is faltering and optimism is the last thing you feel capable of mustering. At these times it's also courageous to stop, let down, and give yourself permission to say:

AFFIRMATION: Today I'm not feeling so brave. I'll give myself a break.

Pray for the dead and fight like hell for the living.
— "MOTHER" MARY JONES

Sage advice in the irreverent tradition of Mother Jones.

We cannot resurrect the dead; we can only bless them in memory and pray that they are peaceful. We can, however, fight like hell for the living, and that begins with ourselves. It means forcing ourselves to summon the energy to put everything we've got into surviving—and thriving—despite our loss. It means putting lots of love and commitment into our relationships that continue to sustain us. Sometimes it means literally pushing ourselves out of bed, out the door, to an event or gathering that may energize us if only we can get ourselves going.

And sometimes it means staying put, letting ourselves grieve a bit more until we're ready to gather our strength and say:

AFFIRMATION: I'm fighting like hell.

I was no more interested in sex than I was in learning to hang-glide.

—DR. JOYCE BROTHERS

It may take a long, long time before you feel even the slightest interest in sex. At best your libido may barely limp along; many widows say their sex drive is virtually nonexistent.

If your spouse suffered a long illness prior to death, your sex life may have ground to a standstill some time ago. Your sexual appetite *will* return; how you nourish yourself will depend on what romantic twists and turns your life takes over the next few years.

It's all part of the healing process. As your lust for life revives, so will your appetite for all things pleasurable and life-affirming. Meanwhile body massages, luxurious bubble baths, and warm bear hugs are others ways of feeling sensual and loved.

AFFIRMATION: My sexuality will eventually be rekindled.

I remember in the beginning obsessing about plans for the next weekend before this one was even over.
                                                    —XENIA ROSE

Thank God It's Friday has turned into Oh, No! Another Long, Lonely Weekend Looming Ahead.

Weekends are just plain hard. One of the perks of marriage was the security of counting on social engagements—and a playmate—with whom to pass the time. Unless we want to rattle around the house or stare at the television, it's important to fill our dance card proactively.

Get on the phone and plan something to look forward to for the next two weekends. Better to have too many options; you can always cancel if you change your mind. In time you may look forward to freedom and solitude. But for now distraction and company may well be the order of the day. Start now by completing the following sentences:

AFFIRMATION: This weekend I have plans to . . .
Next weekend I have plans to . . .

Birthdays and wedding anniversaries can be especially emotionally laden. For years you've carefully chosen a gift, the perfect card, a special treat to acknowledge these meaningful passages.

Our urge to express loving sentiments doesn't diminish with death. In the following space acknowledge his birthday, your anniversary, Valentine's Day, or any other holidays:

My Dearest_____,

On this special occasion I want you to know that . . .

I figured out I'm really angry at him for not staying around to finish the fight.

—WOMAN IN GRIEF GROUP

What an honest statement! And what a real sentiment shared by so many widows who feel cheated by their partner's departure in the middle of a fight.

As Esther, a fifty-two-year-old recently widowed woman said, "Bill and I had started therapy a few months before his cancer was diagnosed. We were making real progress in resolving our marital problems when we had to stop.

"Now what am I supposed to do with *my* feelings?" Esther asked the group facilitator. The answer was simple and direct: "Finish the fight on your own."

For Esther that meant returning to counseling in an effort to resolve her anger at being left to complete the process. Whether it's being angry that he "left" in the middle of a fight or that he left before finishing a project we were mutually involved in, the task remains the same: to let our anger out so that we can get on with what remains to be done.

AFFIRMATION: I will go the rest of the way on my own.

The bill collectors call and I just cry on the phone.
—STEPHANIE ERICCSON

Our spouse's death may have left us financially struggling, in extreme cases on the verge of bankruptcy.

If this doesn't apply to you, give thanks that you are economically stable and give yourself credit for the ways in which you helped secure your future. If, however, your mate's death has caused a financial crisis, here are a few suggestions:

- Try to not feel ashamed or embarrassed. Beating yourself up will only add to the stress.
- Make an appointment with a financial adviser (they're listed in the Yellow Pages) so that you can establish a debt-repayment plan.
- Invest in an answering machine. You *don't* have to subject yourself to abusive calls from creditors.

Financial debt is one of the worst casualties of widowhood. Cry when you need to, but be sure to take care of business as soon as possible.

AFFIRMATION: I can handle all of my financial obligations in due time.

Have You Settled Any and All Outstanding Debts?

You may have incurred short- or long-term financial debt, especially if your husband's illness required substantial medical care. This is one thing you don't need hanging over your head, so begin formulating whatever payment plan will settle your obligations or at least get you on the right road.

At times you may feel resentful at the financial burden resulting from your husband's death. The best antidote is action: get on the phone with your insurance carrier and your financial adviser and make a workable repayment plan that will ease your mind.

Do not make any important changes or decisions for at least a year.

—ALL WIDOWS

It's tempting to make dramatic changes in the midst of crisis. Selling our home, finding a new job, or a whirlwind courtship and remarriage are ways of trying to seize control—quick fixes—when we feel overwhelmingly out of control.

Resist the urge. Why? Because nine times out of ten impulsive moves motivated by fear and trauma backfire. Our reasoning abilities aren't at their best; we simply don't have enough information and experience to make sound choices when our insides are in a knot and our lives are in turmoil.

If you must make a change, do something that's relatively cheap, repairable, and that doesn't have long-term ramifications. Take a trip, learn how to play the sax, or color your hair. It will achieve similar results without serious regrets.

AFFIRMATION: I will be patient.

Pain is important; how we evade it, how we succumb to it, how we deal with it, how we transcend it.

—AUDRE LORDE

It's human to want to avoid pain at all costs. The fight-or-flight instinct is strong; we struggle to avoid feeling the intensity of our heartbreak and we look for ways to escape.

But it's healthy to fully feel our pain. Fighting it—trying not to cry, trying to talk ourselves out of it—only prolongs the grieving process. Avoidance—through keeping busy, addictive behavior, or other escape mechanisms—is impossible. The more we run, the more it follows and torments us.

Allowing ourselves to surrender to our pain is the only way around it. In the depths of despair we are certain we will never find our way out of the darkness. But on the other side is light. And cleansing. And the knowledge that we have survived.

Our spirits are resilient; the deeper we go, the stronger we emerge.

AFFIRMATION: I have faith that I will get to the other side.

I felt vulnerable, unattractive, unloved, and hideously alone.

—PHILOMENE GATES

We feel shaky and unsure of ourselves; we've lost our center and aren't standing on solid ground.

We may feel insecure about our appearance; even if he hardly ever complimented us, we *knew* that in the eyes of our beloved we were beautiful and sexy.

If ever we needed love, it's now, and the one person with an infinite supply is no longer here to shower us with affection.

All of which makes us feel hideously alone in the world. Will anyone ever take care of us, be attracted to us, love and care for us again?

Maybe yes, maybe no—in the form of a spouse, that is. Meanwhile we need to take stock of the other relationships we can turn to for nurturing and love.

Start now. In the following space write down the names of at least three people you can depend on for support, appreciation, affection, and companionship:

AFFIRMATION:

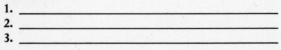

    1. _____

    2. _____

    3. _____

Joy is what happens when we allow ourselves to recognize how good things are.

—MARIANNE WILLIAMSON

Time to count our blessings. Even as we mourn our loss, we can take a moment to acknowledge and appreciate how very much we have.

Take out a piece of paper and write down "Today I am grateful for . . ." finishing the sentence with everything that gives you pleasure, support, and satisfaction. Think about the members of your family who have sustained you during this time. Consider the friends who have been and continue to be there for you in a million different ways. Think about how fortunate you are to have your home, career, community involvements, even your pets and plants— anything and everything that enriches your life.

Expressing gratitude, especially in hard times, is a way of gaining balance and perspective. It's a way of reminding ourselves:

AFFIRMATION: I am so blessed.

> *I become painfully aware that no one is paying me for*
> *all the hours I need to stare into space after a loss.*
> —MARY HAYES-GRIECO

We become anxious at all the time wasted grieving, curled up on the couch with a balled-up handkerchief, staring off into space, reliving the details of his death over and over again.

There are so many other things we should be doing! Yet in truth this is exactly what we must do right now in order to heal and get on with the business of life. The laundry may pile up and social and work appointments may be put on hold until we are in a position to be productive.

This is the "work" of mourning, and while there is no tangible compensation, the actual payment is considerable. If we give ourselves all the time we need, we come out on the other side, rested and ready to resume our worldly responsibilities. Until then we need to keep pressure to an absolute minimum and remember to be easy on ourselves.

AFFIRMATION: I will do the necessary work of grieving, trusting that I will emerge whole and replenished.

In general I am afraid of just about everything: car-jackings, drive-by shootings, bricks and rocks being thrown from freeway overpasses.

— RUTH COUGHLIN

When the worst has happened, we feel immensely vulnerable to danger. Our world has literally fallen apart; our trust in the universe is permanently shaken. Rather than panicking or feeling ashamed of our fears, we can take care of ourselves by turning to friends who can reassure us, taking practical steps to protect ourselves, finding ways to feel relatively safe and secure.

We can—and must—also remember that we have survived. We have learned what we're made of, we have cultivated strategies for overcoming fear. In the face of one of the most devastating of tragedies, we have come through with strength and courage that we can count on in the days ahead.

AFFIRMATION: I have learned how much I can handle.

You know you're healing when you can be home alone without feeling that someone is missing.
—ANNE HOSANSKY

It may take months, even years, before we walk through the front door without calling his name, before we stop half expecting to see him every time we turn a corner, before we stop waiting for him to come home in order for *us* to feel fully and completely at home with ourselves.

This is a later stage of healing. The palpable sense of someone missing may continue for a very, very long time. Some widows even describe feeling as if his ghost is present —an eerie, yet strangely comforting feeling of him hovering in our midst. We may carry on conversations as if he is right in the room; we may even ask his opinions about our haircut or the new dining-room wallpaper, all of which is perfectly natural and *not* a sign that we are losing our minds.

On the contrary our ongoing awareness of his presence is a comfort and a way of remaining connected, until being alone—at home—becomes more comfortable and right.

AFFIRMATION: Someone is missing. And I miss him.

The first time I forced myself to go to a New Year's Eve party alone, I worried about the silliest thing: Whom would I kiss at the stroke of midnight?
                                    —DR. JOYCE BROTHERS

Frankly there's nothing silly about worrying whom you'll kiss at the stroke of midnight. Or under the mistletoe. Or at the moment your child's name is called at graduation.

These are awkward moments during which we feel acutely aware of our loss, singularly alone when everyone around us seems coupled.

So what do we do? For one thing it helps to anticipate these situations so that we won't be caught off guard. For example after my divorce I went to temple one night and at the end of the service found myself standing there alone as all the other couples turned to one another, said "Good Shabbos," and kissed. The next time I went, I made sure I invited a friend, someone I could hug immediately following the benediction.

However, there *are* places we just might not be ready for, situations in which being alone causes more pain than pleasure. In which case there's no need to set ourselves up. Sometimes we need to push ourselves out the door; other times we need to sit tight until a better time.

AFFIRMATION: I'll carefully choose how and with whom I socialize right now.

I compared every man I met with my husband, and none of them measured up.

—RACHEL J.

No one ever will. And that's *exactly* the way it should be!

Naturally we compare our spouse to other potential male suitors; and of course they all fall short. The love we've shared, the multitude of experiences, the comfort and trust we've built over years and years can't possibly be replaced in the company of another man, no matter how wonderful he is.

In many ways this is all about timing. When we're not yet ready to let another man in, we'll find a million reasons why he's not good enough—all of which come down to: He just doesn't hold a candle to the man I loved. With time we're able to see other men in a whole new light, appreciating their unique qualities without measuring them against our spouse. We may even be grateful for the differences, without feeling as if we're compromising our standards or in any way being disloyal to the past.

If, over the long haul, we hold our spouse as the standard, we will certainly chase away men who may be wonderful companions, friends, or even someday lovers. And, in doing so, we'll miss having them as part of a wonderful new chapter in our life.

AFFIRMATION: Comparing other men to him is just a way of keeping myself from getting what I need.

During our marriage we may or may not have been aware of and acknowledged the unique ways in which we felt loved by our spouse. Remembering his love fills us with pleasure and sadness, all of which you can express in the following letter:

My Dearest_____,

Let me count the ways you loved me. . . .

The moment of change is the only poem.
—ADRIENNE RICH

Understanding these words requires a significant shift in how we interpret difficult and painful life passages. It's natural to see change, especially when it involves loss, as a negative experience that we'd rather avoid. However, as Adrienne Rich (and most philosophers) explains, it is in the very moment of change that we experience life at its fullest.

Think about the time that has passed since your partner's death. Every aspect of your loss has presented you with new challenges and opportunities. There's nothing easy about it: yet times of transition force us to be more fully alive, more completely who we are.

Perhaps that is the answer to the question Why do bad things have to happen? This is how we learn. This is how we grow.

AFFIRMATION: I celebrate moments of change, trusting they are transformative.

MONTH TEN   **DAY NINE**

Every married woman should ask herself, "If my husband were to die tomorrow, what would I live on?"
                                              —DR. JOYCE BROTHERS

If you've pursued a career and feel confident of your earning power, you may thank your lucky stars—both for the involvement in your work and for the economic security it ensures. If, however, you've spent your life making a home and raising children, without your own independent means of supporting yourself, this may be a very scary transition. Going back to work, especially in midlife or beyond, may be yet another overwhelming challenge you hadn't bargained for; many communities have resource centers that offer vocational counseling for women who are new to or reentering the workforce, a support system worth investigating.

The good news is: working—whether out of choice or out of necessity—can be a welcome distraction, a source of new friendships, and a real confidence builder. Ultimately you may find it's not only a way of making a living, it's a way of making a new life.

AFFIRMATION: I'm taking care of myself.

Have You Changed the Names on All Jointly Held Credit Cards?

Notifying businesses of your new marital status is another thankless task that's best dealt with as soon as possible. Postponing the inevitable only prolongs the pain of receiving phone calls and correspondence in his name.

You might ask a close friend for help in this matter. A simple, signed form letter will do the job.

Vitamins, exercise, fresh air and sunlight will help your body continue to clear through this stress.
—MARY HAYES-GRIECO

So often we forget the basics in the midst of grieving. So here's a reminder: Each of these healing agents strengthens us and makes us more able to deal with the considerable stress we're experiencing right now.

Vitamins are an essential supplement, especially when we're skipping meals or living on junk food. It takes time to get used to dining alone; the simple act of swallowing a vitamin pill is one positive way to keep your energy up.

Exercise is another. If working out is already part of your daily life plan, keep it up! If not, any amount of exercise, whether you join a health club or take a brisk walk around the block, will boost your spirits and enhance your overall well-being. If you do it outside, all the better. Inhaling great big breaths of fresh air keeps us centered and reminds us we're alive. Admiring the trees, staring at the sky, taking in the beauty of gladiolas growing toward the sky—all of these activities reconnect us to the majesty of the universe.

And perhaps, most healing of all, is the radiance of the sun. Allow it to wash over you. Bathe in its comfort. Let it fill you with warmth.

AFFIRMATION: I will try to nourish myself in every possible way.

One of the best ways to meet a new husband is to become involved in grief groups, I am told. Get it? All those widowers.

—RUTH COUGHLIN

Not! In fact, writer Ruth Coughlin goes on to say, "It's impossible for me to imagine any widow or widower traipsing off to a grief group in search of a new companion. . . . To someone who is bereaved, the notion of being out there on the prowl is unthinkable."

Friendships, yes. Attending a grief group is a wonderful way of finding kindred spirits. But as Coughlin implies, this is hardly a singles dating service; in fact anyone who is there specifically for that purpose is doing a great disservice to the trust required for those involved to share their experiences.

In fact one of the best ways of meeting someone new is to go all the way through our grieving, with or without the help of a grief group. Then if and when someone new enters our life, we will be truly ready to say:

AFFIRMATION: Hello. I am ready to know you.

I could tell it was going to be a terrible, horrible, no-good, very bad day.

—JUDITH VIORST

Some mornings we're overcome with dread before we've lifted our head from our pillow. Everything seems an effort; we know it's going to be a terrible, horrible, no-good, very bad day; we wish we could hibernate and start over again tomorrow.

If possible, do it! We have periods of mourning when we just can't get going; we just can't find anything to feel good and hopeful about. If we allow ourselves to hibernate, to immerse ourselves in darkness, we oftentimes emerge with energy and hope.

Knowing how to flow with our feelings, when it's time to lie low, and when it's time to push ourselves out the door helps in the natural process of regeneration.

AFFIRMATION: I'll find the right balance between cocooning myself and coming out to play.

You know you are healing when you give yourself permission to be attracted to other men.

—ANNE HOSANSKY

The operative word here is *permission*. Whereas some widows feel attracted to other men within months of losing their spouse, others go on for years—perhaps forever—without much interest in intimacy.

After years with our beloved, the thought of anyone else capturing our heart may seem impossibly unlikely. Making ourselves attractive to another man may feel disloyal, scary, or just downright weird. And it may simply be too soon. How can we even entertain fantasies when we're still grieving and in pain?

But whether or not we act on it, allowing ourselves to feel open and perhaps even turned on to other men *is* a sign of healing. It is a way of affirming life, of giving ourselves permission to experience pleasure and joy in the company of men, of letting ourselves say yes to our desires without guilt or apology.

AFFIRMATION: Appreciating other men is in no way a betrayal of my love for my late spouse.

*Get out your calendar and write down just how you plan
to spend every Saturday and Sunday for the next month.*
                                        —DR. JOYCE BROTHERS

And that's an order!

All kidding aside, this is a useful exercise; even if you
don't end up doing anything planned, simply having plans on
paper will help ease your fear and anxiety level as to what
the weekends will bring.

In fact this exercise can be expanded to include other
upcoming potentially lonely times. So take out your calendar
and add the following entries:

- How I plan to spend the holidays
- How I plan to spend my birthday
- How I plan to spend our wedding anniversary
- How I plan to spend the anniversary of his death

Planning ahead—getting it down in writing—is a concrete way of making this very important commitment:

**AFFIRMATION: I will actively prepare to keep myself
busy.**

> *One day, in two months or six months or more, you take*
> *a deep breath and say good-bye to your husband.*
> —PHILOMENE GATES

What does it really mean to say good-bye to the love of your life, the person you believed would accompany you on your journey for many, many years ahead?

Here's what it *doesn't* mean: It doesn't mean we forget him, stop loving him, or in any way erase our memories. It doesn't mean we are "finished" with our grieving; it's a long, arduous process in which over time we gradually accept that he is gone.

Rather, saying good-bye simply means we are learning to accept his death—and discovering how to live in the present. Ultimately saying good-bye is a way of saying yes. It's a way of saying:

AFFIRMATION: I miss you, and I'm going on with my life.

MONTH TEN   **DAY SEVENTEEN**

*These days I am better able to remember Bill as he was
before he got sick.*

—RUTH COUGHLIN

Our ability to conjure up memories of our mate before his
sickness and death is yet another significant sign of healing.
At first images of him frail, weak, and gaunt, consume our
memory; we picture him struggling through invasive medical
procedures, propped up in his hospital bed as he approached
and met death. We can hardly recapture images of him as the
robust, healthy man we married.

Gradually a clearer, more complete montage emerges.
Our more recent impressions merge with a lifetime of
mental photographs, bringing our partner's likeness into
proper perspective. Over time we have *all* of him—a vivid
picture of who he was at every stage of our life together.

AFFIRMATION: You are coming back into focus.

> *We fight to hold on to recent memories even as, with a force like gravity, time pulls us away from those who have died.*
>
> —MICHAEL DORRIS

We live and relive every detail of him: the sound of his voice, the smell of his shoulders fresh from a shower, the incredible moments of tenderness in the days leading up to his death.

Holding fast to our vivid memories, keeping them foremost in our minds, keeps him from fading away. We despair of forgetting, of his memory gradually becoming hazy in the passage of time.

As the once-sharp edges lose their outline, we are left with softer, blurrier, watercolor images. Impressions replace details. His memory lives on.

AFFIRMATION: Time can't take you away.

How often—will it be for always?—how often will the vast emptiness astonish me like a complete novelty and make me say, "I never realized my loss until this moment."

—C. S. LEWIS

It's as if "the same leg is cut off time after time," C. S. Lewis goes on to elaborate, describing the spirallike, endless reexperiencing of anguish he felt following his wife's death.

Women who are farther along the path, who've been widowed four or five years or more, say the spaces between the pain get bigger and bigger. To be sure, our feelings of loss recur, first on a moment-to-moment basis, then hourly, then daily, then gradually greater spaces of time elapse when we feel relatively peaceful with life as it is.

Emotional preparation makes it far easier to cope with the pain. When sorrow revisits us, we needn't be astonished nor devastated. We simply continue to endure it, each time with greater confidence that the pain will pass.

AFFIRMATION: Grieving is a long, long process.

Sometimes when someone has died we say, "I feel like they're still here." That's because they are.
—MARIANNE WILLIAMSON

Can you see him? He may visit you in your dreams or daydreams, seemingly within your reach, just long enough for you to glimpse his specter.

Can you hear him? He may speak to you in the quiet of the night, answering your unspoken questions, reassuring you, even guiding you on your way.

Can you feel him? Call him into your presence, invite him to return, if only for a moment, long enough to remember that death is but a physical parting. Spiritually he remains, forever at your side.

AFFIRMATION: I can feel you.

*But these were different tears. This time I was grieving
for his loss, not my own.*

—DR. JOYCE BROTHERS

There's an important distinction between the tears we shed
for ourselves and those we shed on account of our mate.

At first we are overwhelmed with suffering for everything
we've lost. We feel abandoned and lonely. We may struggle
with financial and emotional turmoil. We're left to face the
bills, console our children, and rebuild our lives.

Then a day comes when we realize we are sad for *him*—
for the pain and suffering he endured. For the warm July
sunshine he'll never feel again, for the taste of pistachio ice
cream he'll never again enjoy. For the lost dreams and goals
that will never be realized we weep tears of sadness. And in
doing so, we move one more step closer from self-pity to
surrender, from feeling like a victim to gratitude that our
own life goes on.

**AFFIRMATION: I wish he was here—for both our
sakes.**

The pain still comes in waves—and some of them can be tidal—but they come less constantly.

—ANNE HOSANSKY

Time and again widows describe the grieving process as "two steps forward, one step back." There is no finite beginning and end to our pain; the road is curvy, with twists and turns surprising in their intensity. One day we feel relatively okay, the next we're a puddle of tears. For a week we're paralyzed with grief, then suddenly we're filled with optimism and hope.

None of this happens overnight. The pain gradually subsides, and often the shifts are barely discernible. Only with time and perspective can we see the pattern: Yesterday we ate three meals and actually tasted the food; for the past two weeks we've slept until eight in the morning—a blissful relief; it's been nearly a month since we felt sorry for ourselves; we went to a dinner party and had a good time.

And then the pain returns, and once again we are overcome with our loss. It's nature's way of reminding us of how very, very fortunate we were.

AFFIRMATION: I'll pay attention to the small steps forward.

We left, as we have left all our lovers, as all lovers leave all lovers, much too soon to get the real loving done.
—JUDY GRAHN

We had so much more to give! We may have been "working" on building trust, better communication skills, ways of expressing intimacy in the hope of being better, more loving partners.

Then time ran out. We were still learning, still growing, our relationship still on its way to becoming everything we envisioned.

Which is one more loss to reconcile. Accepting death also means accepting that we were who we were, we gave what we could, we loved as well as we were able at that stage of our life. Nothing is wasted. We go on, continuing to learn and grow, without regret, more able than ever to love.

AFFIRMATION: I gave it my all.

Family are the people we can always come home to.
            —MARVEL HARRISON AND TERRY KELLOGG

We may redefine *family* as a result of our spouse's death. Whom we depend on, whom we invite to holiday gatherings, whom we see as long-term members of our intimate circle changes with the loss of a loved one.

Case in point: My next-door neighbor, Susan's, ex-husband, Bruce, died at thirty-four. In the weeks surrounding his death, funeral, and grieving, Susan felt connected to Bruce's then-girlfriend, Ellen, with whom she has remained in touch, based on their mutual love and loss. For Carol it worked the other way. Her late husband's grown children had barely recognized their marriage, and wanted nothing to do with her once their father had died. Yet Carol remained close to Nate's aging mother, regularly visiting her in the nursing home as long as she lived.

Ultimately "family" are those people with whom we feel deeply connected over time, with whom we can safely say:

AFFIRMATION: In your company I feel at home.

MONTH TEN   DAY TWENTY-FIVE

I am a woman who lost her husband but found herself.
                                              —LYNN CAINE

After each of my divorces I discovered aspects of myself that
had been dormant, buried, or unexplored within the context
of that relationship. Gary was a gourmet cook; only after
leaving him did I realize how much I loved puttering in the
kitchen, not to mention how much I'd learned from all the
years of watching him cook. Since leaving Joey I've recov-
ered my passion for adventure; on several weekends I've
hopped in my car and headed out of town, sometimes alone,
sometimes with friends, but always with excitement at what
beckoned ahead.

   Although there's nothing to celebrate in losing our mate,
we can take pleasure in the ways we are fulfilling our dreams,
knowing he would be proud of who we are becoming.

**AFFIRMATION: I am getting to know myself in new
ways.**

WISHES

> *I am not going to die, I'm going home like a shooting star.*
>
> —SOJOURNER TRUTH

We long for reunion, for the absolute peace of finally returning home.

Reunion is about connection, whether it's merging with one's "Maker" or finding sanctuary within the whole of nature of which we are an integral part. Although I usually think of reunion as a gentle joining, Sojourner Truth's words, circa 1883, describe a jubilant homecoming, bursting through the heavens without hesitation, lighting the entire sky.

Which reminds us to notice each shooting star. Make a wish. Imagine it carrying our beloved home.

AFFIRMATION: When I wish upon a star . . .

Life does not stop for sorrow.

—DOROTHY RILEY

Which is unfortunate. How wonderful if we could be granted a temporary hiatus from daily obligations while we give full attention to our grief. If only we didn't have to worry about paying bills, fix cars, remember the recycling for at least a month following the burial . . .

But life doesn't stop. We can, however, slow it down to the minimum speed limit until we gradually resume our capacity to handle responsibilities. We can lower our expectations and rigorously prioritize what's urgent and what can wait. And we can accept help when offered. One of the best ways a friend or relative can be supportive is by volunteering to help with the day-to-day minutiae that right now are energy draining and difficult to concentrate on.

Mundane tasks can also be a welcome distraction. They keep us grounded in purpose and reality—so long as they're not overwhelming. At times when it all seems like too much, don't hesitate to ask for help.

AFFIRMATION: Please help me with some of the little things.

No time is ever wasted if you have a book along as a companion.

—MARION WRIGHT EDELMAN

An engrossing book is a great companion at night in bed, as a "dining partner" in restaurants, for those long Sunday afternoons when we're not sure how to fill our time.

Losing ourselves in a book serves numerous purposes: We temporarily forget our troubles and we broaden our horizons and are reminded of the bigger world of which we are still a part. Unfortunately we may find it hard to concentrate, reading and rereading the same passages over and over again without anything sinking in.

That's okay. For now a magazine may be all we can concentrate on. Eventually we'll find books trusted bedfellows and friends we can count on to transport us, entertain us, and keep us company when we're alone.

AFFIRMATION: There's nothing like an engrossing book.

The only gift is a portion of yourself.
— JAMES RUSSELL LOWELL

We may take solace in knowing that our spouse's vital organs live on in another. Being an organ donor is a significant act of giving; someone, somewhere is eternally grateful for the piece of our beloved that makes their own life more viable.

"Sometimes when I'm really sad and missing Victor, I think about his heart beating in another human being," says Lydia, who fully supported her husband's decision to be on the donor program. It's some people's way of ensuring their immortality. And in moments of mourning it helps to know that something good has come of our mate's death, that our loss is another person's gain.

AFFIRMATION: My beloved lives on.

*To know even one life has breathed easier because we
have lived—this is to have succeeded.*

—RALPH WALDO EMERSON

How do you measure the success of a life? Not necessarily by
a dying person's assessment. In the final stages leading up to
death your spouse may have taken inventory of his achievements; he may or may not have felt he had lived up to his
potential or achieved all that was possible.

We may have tried to convince him that he had value, that
he needn't burden himself with regret. Whether or not we
succeeded, it's important for us to celebrate his essence, his
achievements, the ways in which we breathed easier because
of his presence—knowing this is what it means to live a
successful life.

**AFFIRMATION: I am proud of all my mate accom-
plished in his lifetime.**

You have two choices: you will become harder or you will become softer.

—MARIANNE WILLIAMSON

Simply put, this is precisely the spiritual challenge of widowhood or any other profound life loss. We can become hard and cynical, mistrustful and self-pitying, building up our armor as a way of preventing hurt again.

Or we can become softer, more yielding, gentler as a result of our experience. The latter is often visible on the faces of those who have survived the loss of a love; their eyes are knowing, their smile an offering of hope; their words are filled with wisdom and generosity of spirit. They have been there, and they want to help others in their journey.

It's a choice. We become harder or we become softer. In our hearts we know the way.

AFFIRMATION: My loss has made me softer and more tender.

ALL-ENCOMPASSING

You were my North, my South, my East, my West.
My workaday week, my Sunday rest.

                     —W. H. AUDEN

These words, included in the funeral service in the film *Four Weddings and a Funeral,* speak volumes about the enormity of our loss.

In many ways our mate was our world. He was our compass, our globe, the map upon which we fashioned our direction and destination.

He was there when we awoke and upon our lying down. An ever-present part of our daily existence, our playmate and companion for our moments of pleasure and rest.

The sun will rise, the moon will set, we will go to work, we will find our rest, but without him the world will be a bit smaller, a little harder to navigate.

AFFIRMATION: You meant the world to me.

Acceptance should not be mistaken for a happy stage.
                                    —ELISABETH KÜBLER-ROSS

Whereas acceptance has been identified as the final stage in
the process of grieving, it mustn't be confused with hope—
which is the final stage of healing.

Just because we accept something doesn't mean we are
happy about it, it just means we have come to terms with
reality. And reality isn't always cause for celebration. On the
contrary, as we come to accept our loss, we may experience
deeper layers of sadness. As reality sinks in, as our beloved's
death becomes an unassailable fact of life, we dive fully into
our pain until we emerge from the stage of acceptance, ready
to move toward the stage of hope, when we can truly say:

**AFFIRMATION: I'm starting to feel touches of opti-
mism.**

CHILDREN

Children should be listened to and allowed to vent their feelings, whether they be guilt, anger or plain sadness.
—ELISABETH KÜBLER-ROSS

When our children are suffering, our instinct is to try to make it better. But often we make it worse—by denying their feelings. By telling them, either subtly or blatantly, to get over it. By trying to convince them that "everything will be all right."

That's because when our children hurt, we hurt. But as I learned from helplessly seeing my children's pain during our divorce, the most loving response is simply to encourage them to express their feelings, no matter how much we want to "fix" them.

Our children will be strengthened by their suffering; we can't intervene, we can't magically make it disappear, but we can be loving witnesses and say:

AFFIRMATION: I know you're hurting. I'm here.

MONTH ELEVEN   **DAY FIVE**

Grasping is our suffering.

—STEPHEN LEVINE

According to Stephen Levine, the author of *Healing into Life and Death,* our suffering comes from our perfectly human desire to hold on to rather than relinquish our beloved.

This is true in many aspects of life; we experience anguish when we desperately want something and can't have it. As soon as we let go—knowing we will survive and perhaps even thrive with or without our mate—our pain is dramatically diminished and we feel a certain measure of peace.

All of which is easier said than done. Our instinct is to hold on tightly to that which we value. The paradox is that letting go is the ultimate act of love. It may be the hardest task of all.

AFFIRMATION: I will cultivate loving detachment.

> *The good thing about masturbation is that you don't
> have to dress up for it.*
>
> —TRUMAN CAPOTE

Even Dr. Ruth can't speak highly enough of the rewards of
self-pleasure, so I feel safe in bringing it up here as a positive
and healthy option.

Masturbation may or may not be part of our regular sexual repertoire; we may have internalized taboos against it—
that it's bad or "dirty"—or else it simply may have been
irrelevant when we were married.

But not only is it fine—in fact it's an act of self-love—it
can also go a long way toward replenishment, which is of top
priority right now. Remember, any way we feed ourselves
helps us heal. In the privacy of our bedroom, where we
don't have to "dress up," we are free to give ourselves
whatever we need.

AFFIRMATION: I give myself the gift of pleasure.

> *Although I do not believe in reincarnation, I convince
> myself this moth is Bill.*
>
> —RUTH C.

There's two ways to look at this: Either we're going crazy or
we're gaining a deepened spiritual awareness as a result of
our loss.

I prefer the latter explanation. Although there's no prov-
ing it, and even thinking it makes us wonder if we're losing
our mind, the idea of reincarnation can seem more realistic
as a result of our experiences of death and grieving, as well
as supernatural phenomena and other mystical explanations
for the hereafter. Having witnessed death up close, we may
undergo a profound shift in our belief in God or a higher
power.

Who's to say? If pondering life's mysteries is part of your
healing process, remain as open as possible. If a butterfly, a
dandelion, or your brand-new grandchild seems to embody
your beloved's spirit, why not! Allow yourself to see him in
whatever form he appears.

**AFFIRMATION: I am open to mystical aspects of the
universe.**

*I dreamed that he had returned in various ways, and
that I did not want him back.*

—JILL TRUMAN

Is this a dream or a nightmare? After all the months of
missing him, he appears in our slumber, and lo and behold
—we have mixed feelings at the thought of having him back.

Horror of horrors, have we stopped loving our mate? *No.*
We've simply moved far enough along in our healing that the
idea of reintegrating him into our current picture of our life
presents an overwhelming emotional dilemma.

Consider the ramifications if suddenly, magically he was
resurrected? How would he fit into the new home we may
have created solely to our own taste? Would he dramatically
disrupt—perhaps even disapprove of—the lifestyle we've
grown accustomed to? We're used to our solitude, our freedom, the choices we've made that he may or may not embrace. And what of the new relationships we've formed in
his absence? Would we face new losses in welcoming him
back into our life?

Ambivalence at the fantasy of having him back reflects
nothing other than our having moved a few paces forward.
Knowing this may make us sad. But we can also feel glad at
the progress we've made.

**AFFIRMATION: I celebrate the ways in which I am
moving forward.**

As the weeks, months, and years go by, we are increasingly aware of the ways in which our mate permanently affected us—in relatively superficial ways, such as teaching us to ski or the best way to sauté onions; and in very significant ways, such as sharing his philosophy of life.

We are grateful for the lessons. And we can tell him so. In the following space compose a letter to your love describing all the ways he has been —and continues to be—your teacher and guide:

My Dearest_____,

    You have taught me so many things. . . .

You don't really get over it; you get used to it.
—ROBERT S. WEISS

I find this distinction remarkably reassuring. We may think that we're supposed to get over our pain, that the goal of our healing is to reach a place where our loss is no longer a tangible part of our life.

In fact healing gradually occurs as a result of accepting and becoming accustomed to our loss—learning to live with our spouse's absence—getting used to who we are without our beloved as we go on with our lives.

"Getting over it" somehow translates into "hurry up," whereas "getting used to it" assumes we are in a process of learning, growing, becoming a new person for whom the past will forever inform the present and the future. Getting over it means forgetting; getting used to our loss means remembering what we've been through and finding creative ways of integrating it into our lives.

AFFIRMATION: I'll never get over it, but I am getting used to it.

"What do you celebrate?" I asked. "Getting better" was the reply. "We celebrate if we are a better, wiser person this year than last."

—MARLO MORGAN

This past year has been difficult; just surviving has been enough of a challenge, without finding reasons to celebrate. But this exchange from the marvelous book *Mutant Message Down Under*—a fictional account of an American woman's amazing four-month odyssey with the Aborigines of Australia —offers a different measure of joy, one that we can readily relate to. If there's one thing—and it may well be the *only* thing—we can genuinely celebrate, it's getting better.

Take a moment to look back on the past twelve months. List five ways in which you have become more loving, more compassionate, and wiser for wear:

AFFIRMATION:

1. _____
2. _____
3. _____
4. _____
5. _____

That day I began to realize that I would, someday, be happy again.

—STEPHANIE ERICCSON

For Stephanie that realization came during Christmas shopping, about five weeks after her husband's death, when she found herself smiling while trying to figure out what gifts to buy her friends.

In no way did this event signify the end of mourning; for many more months the author of *Companion Through the Darkness* spent countless hours immersed in grief. Yet there were occasional reprieves, glimpses of hope and happiness that in her words "came from getting out of myself for a few hours to give to others."

It's important to notice the moments of lightness when we realize that someday we will be happy again. We will never stop missing our mate, but in time we will smile, laugh, look forward to tomorrow, and feel good about being alive.

AFFIRMATION: I will feel happy again.

*Soon my body will drop away from me like a cocoon and
my spirit will fly like a butterfly.*
— "BILL," AS QUOTED BY STEPHEN LEVINE

These words are taken from a letter written by a man with
AIDS. We sense his readiness, perhaps even eagerness, to
shed the outer skin of his being that encapsulates his spirit so
that he can soar.

It's a beautiful metaphor, one worth imagining in moments when we mourn our beloved's death. Perhaps the
shell of his cocoon has merely dropped away, freeing him to
fly away, no longer imprisoned by worldly weight or physical
limitation.

His spirit cannot be contained. Somewhere above, he
soars, wings spread, light as a butterfly.

AFFIRMATION: Fly away, my love.

Close your eyes and try to picture the where-abouts of your mate. Do you imagine his physi-cal being—as you recall him—actually present in some fantasy heaven (or hell)? Do you see him lying motionless in the ground? Do you fantasize his spirit separated from his body, perhaps mani-fested in the lilacs growing in your backyard or in the bluebird perched in the branches outside your window?

In the space below write a letter to your love describing your fantasy of who and where he is today. Begin with these words:

My Dearest_____,

When I close my eyes, I picture you . . .

Travel not only stirs the blood. . . . It also gives strength to the spirit.

—FLORENCE PRAG KAHN

Recently, after a drawn-out illness, Gene, my brother-in-law's father, passed away. Dorothy, his wife of nearly fifty years, planned a trip to New York with a friend, and knowing how much I travel, she came to me for advice, explaining, "I married at age twenty, and Gene and I always traveled together. I've never gone anywhere alone."

Dorothy wanted to know some of the basics: How to hail a cab at La Guardia Airport. How to nab a porter to carry her luggage. How much to tip. And the question I found most poignant, "How do I act as if I know where I'm going so that no one takes advantage of me?"

Her first three questions were easy; the last one made me aware that this journey was a symbolic and courageous leap. It paid off well. Dorothy returned rejuvenated, more confident for having navigated the ropes, her spirit strengthened by knowing she could make it—and then some—on her own.

AFFIRMATION: I can get around on my own.

To do good things in the world, first you must know who you are and what gives meaning to your life.
—Paula P. Brownlee

Important life passages are a terrific time to reexamine our values and recommit to making a difference in the world. Charitable giving serves two purposes: It offers meaningful distraction and it enables us to give something back.

Volunteer work is somewhat contingent on schedules. If your career is demanding, you may have limited time and resources, but even one hour a week can be an affordable and empowering way to add meaning to your existence. If your mate's death has left you looking for ways to fill time, charitable work may be just the thing. Some widows find it fulfilling to raise money for the specific illness their spouse succumbed to. Participating in church or synagogue activities; collecting for your neighborhood cancer or heart fund; volunteering at a food shelf, battered-women's shelter, or high-risk nursery are all ways of getting your mind off your troubles and helping others in need.

It simply feels good to give. And we get so very, very much in return.

AFFIRMATION: Here's one way I can give:_____.

Now I am alone with no husband to care for, and they are grown up and have busy lives.

—PHILOMENE GATES

Although our grown children, too, are grieving, they may not be readily available for company and commiseration. They've lost their father, but their schedules are already overflowing with stressful careers, young kids, and numerous other demands.

But the loss of our mate has left our days empty, our nights long, and our weekends wide open; although it's tempting to turn to our children, we have to accept their time limits, which are no reflection of their love. After all we've given them, it's natural to expect them to be at our beck and call. But the more we pressure them, the worse they—and we—feel.

It's up to us to cultivate other activities and relationships so that we don't feel dependent on our children. They can be part of—but not all of—our lives.

AFFIRMATION: My children have their own lives to live.

I enter the last trimester of the first year of Len's death.
                                        —REBECCA RICE

Pregnancy is an apt metaphor for the first nine months of bereavement: In the first trimester most widows walk around in a state of disbelief, exhausted and overwhelmed, which is similar to how expectant mothers feel and act. In the second trimester widows typically begin the process of acceptance; likewise reality sinks in as pregnant women feel their baby kick and see their belly grow. The last trimester is marked by a mixture of excitement, trepidation, and anticipation: Widows begin to open themselves to creating a new life, and pregnant women prepare themselves for labor and delivery.

Preparation for birth, just like recovery from mourning, is a journey of creation. Each stage is another step toward rebirth.

AFFIRMATION: I am giving birth to a new self.

I was not at her bedside that final day.
                                              —GALWAY KINNELL

We desperately wanted to be right there when he died. Some of us made it, while others, for reasons beyond our control, missed the actual moment of his death, for which we feel regret and perhaps guilt.

If we weren't at our beloved's bedside, we may be angry at the hospital for failing to notify us on time, or angry at ourselves for having gone to the hospital dining room after hours of sitting vigil and being summoned just after the fact. We may worry that he suffered more because we weren't there; we may castigate ourselves for failing him when he needed us most.

We can't rewind the tape, we can't reverse the circumstances. We can, however, remember all the minutes, hours, days, and weeks we were heroically at his side, all the times we comforted him, advocated on his behalf, held his hand up until the moment of death.

AFFIRMATION: I was there when it mattered.

Would I bring her back to life if I could do it? I would not.

—MARK TWAIN

After hearing choruses of widows say, "I'd move heaven and earth to have him back," these words by Mark Twain took me aback. Could he have meant that he preferred life without his deceased wife, that he didn't miss her and didn't grieve her death?

No. As he continues, "In her loss I am almost bankrupt and my life is a bitterness, but I am content—because she has been enriched with that most precious of all gifts—death."

What altruistic love is required to not only accept but celebrate our beloved's passing and all the positive things it represents—the release from pain, the freedom from worldly responsibilities, and perhaps, depending on our religious beliefs, a piece of heaven inhabited by our spouse? It's not easy to be joyous about our loss. But even as we mourn, we slowly move toward being able to utter the words:

AFFIRMATION: In my love I release you.

This one's a leap. Finding reasons to be joyous about our mate's death may be more than we're ready for; if so, return to this exercise in a few weeks or months.

If, however, you're ready, write a letter to your love, telling him ways in which you are happy for *him,* ways in which you feel his death has freed him from suffering, ways in which you trust he is better off. You might begin with these words:

My Dearest_____,

    As much as I miss you, I rejoice that . . .

I'll never marry again.

—MANY WIDOWS

For some of us this may be a true statement based on inner conviction born of considerable soul-searching and self-awareness.

Others may make this resolution out of a bitterness and fear that will gradually dissipate with time. We may be unwilling to risk abandonment ever again; we may be afraid that a new relationship constitutes a betrayal of our commitment to our late spouse, or that it could never compare, in which case why bother?

We may or may not choose to become romantically involved, but ultimately what matters is to *choose*—to actively engage or not—because it suits and satisfies us, rather than out of the need to protect ourselves from hurt.

Absolutes are a form of self-entrapment. As we heal, we give ourselves the freedom and flexibility to be open to change.

AFFIRMATION: I'll keep an open mind.

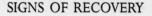

I was coming back to life in very small ways.
                                    —XENIA ROSE

"I stopped in my lobby to play with a small child and noticed a smile on my face," recalls Xenia Rose, illustrating the moment in which she began to reawaken following her husband's death.

Being widowed means that a part of us has died; it takes time to recover, to resurrect hope.

But it will happen—and you may already be aware of the signs. Notice the small ways in which you are gradually coming back to life: when you're surprised by a smile on your own face; when a dinner invitation seems appealing rather than obligatory; when instead of making you burst into tears, the sight of a couple holding hands makes you feel happy inside.

These are brief reprieves—and they are meaningful reminders that the constant weight of mourning will lift as slowly but surely your energy and enthusiasm return.

AFFIRMATION: I am aware of the small signs of recovery.

COMPASSION

Compassion is healing; we are each other's physicians.
—OLIVER SACHS

We can attend grief groups, professional counseling, or psychotherapy, or seek guidance from a minister or rabbi—any or all of which may facilitate our healing.

But as famed neurologist and healer Oliver Sachs points out, the compassion we give, one human being to another, is another important way in which we mend. A scene from the movie *Awakenings,* based on Sachs's work with patients suffering from Parkinson's disease, beautifully illustrates this point. The main character, played by Robert De Niro, has reached a stage in his illness where he is perpetually contorted with uncontrollably grotesque spasms and tics. He meets a lovely young woman who, in an inspired moment, leads him in a slow waltz around the hospital cafeteria. As her arms encircle him, he slowly, imperceptibly dances, his dignity restored by simple human contact far more powerful than anything modern medicine has to offer.

So we, too, in our healing, need compassion. And human touch. Someone who silently reaches out and steadies us until we are fully back on our feet.

AFFIRMATION: Touch me.

Have You Acknowledged All Cards, Donations, and Other Charitable Contributions?

This, too, can seem an overwhelming task; on the one hand it's comforting to acknowledge all expressions of condolence: on the other hand doing so requires energy and focus, which we're probably in short supply of.

So proceed slowly, perhaps by tackling a half dozen a day. Some women find it helpful to purchase preprinted thank-you cards, while others prefer to craft a special message to each person who expressed his or her sympathy. However you approach this, take your time. No one expects immediate replies; give yourself ample time to complete this emotional task.

It's like a slow recovery from a sickness, this recovery on one's self.

—TOBY TALBOT

Putting our grieving into the context of illness is useful in two ways: It helps legitimize the ways in which we are out of balance and out of sorts, and it forces us to treat ourselves gently, caring for our ailment as we would if we were suffering a physical malaise.

Because our "illness" is emotional rather than physical, we may downplay its significance or resist treating ourselves with kid gloves. But just as we must heal our physical wounds, we must attend to our soul's sickness—with rest, nourishment, and visits to healers when needed.

Whether it's our body or our spirit, the Rx is the same: We lovingly, patiently nurse ourselves toward health.

AFFIRMATION: I gently minister to my ailing soul.

MONTH ELEVEN   **DAY TWENTY-SEVEN**

*Let us remember that there is a better world, in which it
is all day, a day that stretches for eternity.*
                                        —MILTON STEINBERG

Those of us who are religiously inclined may take comfort in
the concept of an afterworld—an eternal resting-place in
which there is no suffering, only abundant love and serenity.

If we reject—or simply can't conceive of—an afterworld,
we may imagine our mate permanently asleep or uncon-
scious, which in its own way represents absence of pain and
eternal peace.

Whether we fantasize opulent feasts and angels' serenades
or draw a blank, we can take comfort in knowing that our
beloved is forever free of earthly tribulations and physical
disease, which may have been a constant companion leading
to death. Perhaps there is a better world beyond; perhaps
there is only the one in which we mortals reside, but either
way our beloved is finally out of pain.

AFFIRMATION: May you rest in peace.

> Epitaph: *"It's always a beautiful day in this neighbor-hood."*
>
> —MISTER ROGERS

This quote made me laugh. I like the idea that after death it will always be a beautiful day in the neighborhood—the sun will shine, the temperature will be perfect, there will be no crime, and neighbors will smile in passing.

Although what actually happens postdeath remains a mystery, our healing can be hastened through a positive outlook. If it helps, imagine your beloved awakening in "heaven," opening the front door to fetch the morning paper, stretching his arms, looking up at the sky, and smiling to himself as he says:

AFFIRMATION: What a beautiful day it is today.

I would be reading in bed and come across a fact or an idea that fascinated me and turn automatically to share it with him.

—DR. JOYCE BROTHERS

. . . only to be reminded—again—of the immensity of my loss," says Joyce Brothers in her memoir, *Widow,* written just six months after her husband, Milt, died of a brain tumor.

Again and again we are faced with our loss. After so many years everywhere we turn—a song on the radio, a brochure from a country inn we'd visited, the perennials popping up in the garden we planted together—everything evokes intensely bittersweet memories. Without thinking, we reach out to share, then remember he's no longer there. Often it's the little things: We cut out a coupon for his favorite cereal or memorize a funny bumper sticker to tell him about. Marie, a widow of just one year, says, "After David died, the hardest thing was going to family dinners and not being able to laugh about all my crazy relatives afterward."

There is simply no replacing our very best friend. It may take months, even years, before we stop turning to him to say, "Honey, listen to this. . . ." Who knows? He just may be listening.

AFFIRMATION: Honey, have I told you . . . ?

We're accustomed to relying on our mate for advice, particularly when it comes to important decisions: whether or not to invest in the stock market, the ramifications of taking a promotion or changing jobs, the best strategy for dealing with parenting challenges.

Whether or not he's capable of a reply, it's helpful to put our questions on paper. In doing so, we may be surprised at how well we know him and what he would say. So go ahead and ask his advice, beginning with the words:

My Dearest_____,

What's your opinion about . . . ?

MONTH TWELVE   **DAY ONE**

Little by little you are slipping away from me.
                                        —JILL TRUMAN

We are torn between hanging on and letting go, between wanting time to stand still so that we can remain intensely connected to our love and our loss, and wanting to free ourselves to move on and rebuild our lives.

At first we fiercely resist any mention of tomorrow—and all the tomorrows without him—each one an assault against our aching hearts. With the passage of time we begin lovingly to loosen our grasp.

Ultimately healing means loving him—and ourselves—enough to relinquish our hold. Our beloved slowly slips away, little by little, like the last luminous rays of twilight before the setting sun as we stare into the darkened sky.

And each glorious sunrise beckons us to greet the new day, facing the future as yesterday slowly fades into the distance.

AFFIRMATION: Slip away from me slowly, my love.

WARMTH

*Do you know how many blankets it takes to replace a
husband?*

—YIDDISH SAYING

Too many to count: flannel blankets wrapped around us like
a cocoon; heated blankets tucked up to our chin; heavy
goose-down comforters providing the warmth and safety we
felt cradled in his arms.

And still we shiver. Because there is simply no replacing
our mate, no way of recovering the warmth and comfort of
him slumbering at our side. For now we settle for poor
substitutes: a soft and fuzzy teddy bear, extra pillows, a
warm cup of cocoa on the nightstand. Here in bed our loss
cuts to the core. He was our blanket, our comforter, our
companion in the night. For this there is no replacement. We
can only say:

AFFIRMATION: I will find a way to stay warm.

The ultimate goal of the grief work is to be able to remember without emotional pain.
                                        —ELISABETH KÜBLER-ROSS

Kübler-Ross makes an important distinction between painful recollection and fond remembrance.

The first is what marks earlier stages of grieving; every time we think of our mate, we are filled with sadness and longing. Gradually our recollections are less painful and more pleasurable. We can imagine his face without feeling tears flow down our own; every memory isn't instantly followed by the horrible realization that he's gone.

It makes perfect sense that the capacity to remember our mate without it hurting is the ultimate goal of our healing. With time we will embrace our memories without it hurting quite so much.

AFFIRMATION: I wait for the time when I can remember you without feeling so much loss.

MAINTENANCE

I sit here in this big house by myself trying to sew. But what good is sewing gon do? What good is anything?
—ALICE WALKER

Nothing seems worth bothering with, so why bother? No one will care if we eat a balanced meal or graze on a bag of Chee•tos; no one will notice whether the socks are darned or the bathroom curtains match or the newspapers are put out for recycling.

It's true. No one cares, so *we* have to care. It's a matter of dignity. And it's a matter of survival. Besides, we have to keep busy doing something, so we may as well make it worthwhile. We don't have to get excited about anything, but we *do* have to maintain the basics, such as feeding ourselves, keeping our home relatively orderly, so that we don't add extra chaos to the existing crisis.

And there's another plus to productive work: When we're most in despair, it's empowering to get something—anything—done. Every small task connected to real life helps keep us from giving up.

AFFIRMATION: I keep on keeping on.

I tell my eighteen-year-old son that it takes a man to cry.

—WILLARD K. KOHN

During the Gulf War General Norman Schwarzkopf was interviewed by Barbara Walters. I expected a macho tough guy, but instead, tears rolling down his face, he said, on national television, "Real men cry."

I've always been grateful for that media moment. It's one I plan to repeat to my ten-year-old when he's old enough to understand that being able to weep isn't a sign of weakness but a true measure of strength.

Those of us with children do well to encourage their tears in mourning their father. If we can cry with them or in front of them, if we can hold them closely as they weep, we give them the greatest gift of all: permission to express their raw, real pain.

AFFIRMATION: Go ahead and cry, my darlings.

> *They were more whole, more healed at the moment of their dying than at any other time of their life.*
> —STEPHEN LEVINE

We may have watched as our spouse underwent a profound spiritual transformation in preparation for his death. He may have come to a place of peace and acceptance. He may have forgiven himself and others, reconciling long-standing conflicts and lifelong wounds. As he readied himself to let go, he may have experienced a renewed appreciation of beauty: he may even have understood the meaning of existence, an epiphany often reserved for those on the verge of death.

This is not a universal reality; unfortunately some of us may have witnessed our dying spouse's wrenching and failed attempt to make peace before taking his last breath. In these cases we can only hope and pray that death has brought comfort. And if we were fortunate to observe our beloved release his hold on this world whole and healed, then we can give thanks that:

AFFIRMATION: He found peace in his final moments.

You and I ought not to die before we have explained ourselves to each other.

—JOHN ADAMS

We regret that our beloved exited before the final act of our love story, before we were able to fully make ourselves known.

There are things we wish we could have—would have—clarified about ourselves, our actions, misunderstandings that needlessly estranged us, when a simple explanation would have made all the difference in the world.

But we didn't. Or we couldn't. We may have censored ourselves for fear of disapproval. We may not have had the time or patience to improve communication, to say, "Please listen, I want you to understand who I am and how I feel." And for this we are sorry. Sorry that we couldn't have understood each other perfectly. Sorry that in some ways, we will always remain a mystery to one another.

AFFIRMATION: I wish I had had more time to know you.

You may still feel burdened by things you wish you could explain about yourself to your mate: choices you made that mystified him, words you spoke that bewildered him, aspects of your personality that left him groping in the dark. Here's a way to enlighten him: In the following space compose a letter in which you explain all the "question marks" once and for all, with these words:

My Dearest_____,

    Let me try again to help you understand. . . .

MONTH TWELVE   **DAY NINE**

"Did you ever stop and consider that maybe you loved him too much?" another person asks.

—RUTH COUGHLIN

This infuriates me! How dare anyone suggest that we have caused our own grief by loving our mate too much?

It's impossible to love too much. If anything, we may question whether we loved our spouse nearly enough, which now we are helpless to rectify. Especially in retrospect, we are intensely aware of the ways in which we wish we'd given more.

This sort of comment is inherently disrespectful. Implying that we were overly attached is simply other people's attempts to diminish their discomfort by trying to talk us out of our pain. But our sorrow is a measure of our devotion. We've earned it by loving him just right.

AFFIRMATION: I will try to shrug off insensitive comments.

When you're sad, learn something.

—MERLIN

I've always loved these simple words, taken from the story of King Arthur.

Early in our mourning process our sadness is all-encompassing; we're flooded with sorrow that makes it impossible to think of anything else. But there comes a point when our lingering sadness becomes incapacitating, when it's time to do something hopeful and empowering.

Then, as Merlin the Magician says, we can learn something new. We can focus our energy on personal growth, whether it's losing ourselves in a book, a class, an activity, or any other hobby that is challenging and stimulating.

Learning something new heals us by helping us feel more alive. It's another way of saying:

AFFIRMATION: Here's a reason to get up in the morning.

*There is a T-shirt I like that says, "Behind every suc-
cessful woman is herself."*

—DOLORES HUERTA

Especially if we are in our sixties or older, we may have
spent years being "the woman behind the man," supporting
our husband's career rather than pursuing our own ambitions
and goals.

Now we have the opportunity to focus on ourselves,
which is both frightening and exciting. We may not know
where to start; we may feel lost and adrift, needing him to
anchor us as we take sail. And we may feel exhilarated at our
newfound freedom. We can do anything, but—and it's a big
but—we will have to do it for ourselves, by ourselves, providing the wind beneath our own wings.

There is nothing holding us back if we're willing fully to
invest in our own hopes and dreams.

AFFIRMATION: Let's go!

I am learning to live without a man as the center of my life, without orbiting around him.

—CATHLEEN ROUNTREE

As we shift our focus from being a wife to being a widow, we are forced to learn how to live happily without the security of a partner.

Everything has to be redefined: our identity reframed, our lifestyle reexamined, the very meaning of our existence called into question now that we are a galaxy of one.

Another challenge—another opportunity revealed as we move through the grieving process. At first we can only think of how lost we are without him. Gradually we begin orbiting around ourselves, comfortable with being the center of our own existence. We learn—in part because the call to independence is exciting, in part because we have no other choice—to live a fulfilling life, with ourselves, *for* ourselves.

AFFIRMATION: I am the center of my own life.

Death is the sole equality on Earth.

—PHILLIP J. BAILEY

Paradoxically being widowed both isolates and connects us to the whole human race.

During the long hours sitting vigil in the hospital visitors' lounge, we may have witnessed the intimate details of other families suffering, shared other women's struggle to cope with their husband's death. As we made funeral arrangements, buried our beloved, and throughout our grieving, we came to realize that death is the great equalizer; our empathy and compassion for others—who will inevitably share our experience—grows.

All mortal souls are subject to death; no one is exempt from loss and grieving. Knowing this inspires us to reach across the gulf, to comfort others in pain.

AFFIRMATION: All men are created equal.

Time goes on and we continue changing once our spouse is deceased. It's hard to accept that he's not privy to who we are becoming: We've colored our hair red, we've taken up the guitar; we've joined a fellowship at church and met so many nice, interesting people.

Part of grieving is accepting the aspects of ourselves he will never know. But we can tell him. In the following space let your mate know all the ways in which you have changed and continue to change since he last saw you.

My Dearest_____,

   You'd hardly recognize me! I've learned to . . .

Hard is life for him who lives on for the sake of his beloved ones.

—KAHLIL GIBRAN

At first we are so anguished, our only reason for living is to be there for our children and perhaps our friends.

"I didn't want to go on, yet I couldn't bear the thought of leaving my daughter an orphan," says Gail, whose husband died at forty-eight, leaving her to raise their twelve-year-old child. "If it weren't for my friends—our mutual friends— I'd probably give up," agrees Ellen, explaining, "It seems selfish to put them through another tragedy on the heels of my husband's death."

Pushing ourselves to survive for the sake of others is a double-edged sword. On the one hand we are grateful we have something to live for. On the other hand martyrdom carries its price; ultimately we must find reasons to carry on for our own sake, or we will feel permanently resentful.

In fact there's nothing selfless about it. If living for others right now inspires and motivates us, then we owe *them* a debt of gratitude. To ourselves—or directly to our loved ones— we can say:

AFFIRMATION: Thank you for needing me right now.

DISILLUSIONMENT

> *"Nobody gets in to see the Wizard. Not no way, not no how."*
>
> —L. FRANK BAUM

In our grief we seek wisdom, turning to authority figures—doctors, healers, spiritual advisers—who will unlock the key to life, death, and, most importantly, the meaning of our tragedy.

And we're forced to accept one of the most sobering realities of adulthood: There are no absolute truths; no Yellow Brick Road that will transport us beyond our pain; no magical, mystical answers to the questions that haunt us.

In short nobody gets in to see the Wizard. Not no way. Not no how. But as we strip away another illusion—the illusion of external authority—we look inward—where we rediscover that we ourselves have the brains, the courage, the heart, the wisdom to find our way home.

AFFIRMATION: There's no place like home.

The deeper the sorrow, the less tongue it has.
—THE TALMUD

We're encouraged to talk about our bereavement, to process the details of our experience, to analyze our pain, the insights we've gained as a result of our suffering, in short to express our innermost feelings about what we're going through.

If we're silent, unwilling, or disinterested in verbalizing our feelings, we may be accused of denial, of going underground as escape, of suppressing our sorrow, which is commonly construed as unhealthy and self-destructive.

But as the Talmud wisely counsels, our sorrow may be so profound as to transcend words; silence can be a truer expression and a more replenishing state of being than all the "I feels" and "I'm trying to understands" we can possibly articulate.

Don't feel pressured by anyone's need for you to talk. Silence can be as healing—sometimes even more so—as words.

AFFIRMATION: I don't have to talk about it if I don't feel like it.

He had ceased to meet us in particular places in order to meet us everywhere.

—C. S. LEWIS

We continue to miss his physical presence: across the breakfast table, his arm protectively draped over our shoulder at a dinner party, his warm body snuggled close as we sleep.

Yet, as C. S. Lewis suggests, whereas our beloved has ceased to meet us in the particular places we are accustomed to, perhaps he is all around us, ever present in death.

It's a lovely concept, worth imagining. Close your eyes and picture your husband hovering about, perched on the windowsill, floating in your coffee cup, waving at you from the top branches of a tree.

Perhaps in losing him it's possible to find him, to feel his spirit with us wherever we go.

AFFIRMATION: Now he is part of everything.

I am alone with the beating of my heart.

—LUI CHI

And we are alone with our heartbreak. Being widowed has taught us one of life's hardest and most profound lessons: Ultimately each of us is alone. We are connected to one another, we feel intimate and at times understood. We love and feel loved. Yet in the final analysis our pain is our own, just as our joy, even as we try to describe it, can't entirely be put into words.

Perhaps *separate* is a better word than *alone;* experiencing our utter individuality, our inalienable, solitary status is empowering. We realize we can choose closeness and communion as well as solitude, knowing that we are strong enough to stand firmly on our own, listening to the beating of our heart.

AFFIRMATION: I am separate and whole unto myself.

In search of my mother's garden, I found my own.
                        —ALICE WALKER

Depending on our age, we may have widowed mothers or
mothers-in-law with whom to commiserate and seek guidance. Just as we may have rediscovered a garden of wisdom
and empathy with our mothers during pregnancy, now we
can seek the wisdom of their experience in having been
through a similar loss.

Some of their advice may be helpful ("My mom, who's
eighty-one, remarried last year, which has been an inspiration to me!" says Betsy.) Some of Mom's advice may leave
us feeling as resentful as teenagers whose mothers "just
don't understand," as Georgia experienced when her widowed mother castigated her for wearing colorful clothing to
the funeral. "I deliberately wore my husband, Ivan's, favorite
purple dress," says Georgia, "and my mother still hasn't let
me forget it."

Whether or not we take their advice to heart, bonding
with our mothers, connecting through this shared experience, can be nourishing and healing.

**AFFIRMATION: I could use a little mothering right
now.**

MONTH TWELVE   **DAY TWENTY-ONE**

We are in a seemingly perpetual state of longing.
—STEPHANIE ERICCSON

. . . to touch his hand, to hear his voice, to share the sunset—in hundreds of big and little ways we long for what we no longer can have.

Knowing we can't have what we want doesn't make the longing go away. If anything, it's intensified. And we feel powerless. No matter how much we want him, there's nothing we can do. We'd go to the ends of the earth if it would make a difference, but this one is absolutely out of our control.

And so we learn to live with unrequited longing. With a hunger so intense, we feel as if we'll never again feel content. But we will. Our longing will take new forms, and we will, once again, give and receive love. We may never stop longing to be reunited with our beloved, but we will begin to nourish ourselves in new, perhaps surprisingly nice ways.

AFFIRMATION: I long to be reunited with you.

IMMORTALITY

The body is mortal, but he who dwells in the body is immortal and immeasurable.

—SRI KRISHNA

Our physical shell wears out; it is an inevitable part of the human condition, one we are all subject to.

But the spirit lives on. In moments of missing our mate it helps to recognize the ways in which he is immortal: in his scent, his words, his influences that linger on; in the noble acts and good deeds that have touched the lives of others ("He was a good man," they say, and we appreciate that others share our memories); in our beautiful children, a piece of immortality in which our love is eternally evident.

We cannot hold on to the fragile shell that contained his spirit. We can, however, take comfort in feeling his powerful essence—immortal, immeasurable, and infinitely present.

AFFIRMATION: I cannot see you, touch you, hear you, yet I know you are still here.

MONTH TWELVE   **DAY TWENTY-THREE**

Death and taxes and childbirth! There's never a convenient time for any of them!

—MARGARET MITCHELL

Concerned friends offer condolences, trying to soften the blow: "It was a blessing. Thank God he's no longer in pain." Or "At least he didn't suffer." Or "How fortunate he got to see his brand-new granddaughter before he died."

But it's small comfort at best. Even when true, these comments feel inherently disrespectful; there's nothing convenient or blessed about our loss—no matter when or how he died, we miss him dearly.

If we've learned anything, it's that timing is strictly out of our control. We may or may not be able to make sense of the cosmic timetable; all we can do is say:

AFFIRMATION: I accept my beloved's death, even though I may not understand it.

Have You Taken Care of Your Taxes?

Traditionally this is one area husbands have typically taken care of. Although it isn't true of all widows, for many, meeting the April 15th deadline is another mountain to climb.

If this applies to you, get started. If you already have a CPA, make an appointment so that you know what information to supply. Or ask friends to recommend a few different accountants, interview them, and decide whom you are most comfortable with.

Taxes can be a real burden. Dealing with them promptly constitutes another step toward taking responsibility for your life.

I desire no future that will break the ties of the past.
— GEORGE ELIOT

As we begin to rebuild our future, we are loath to let go of the past. And we needn't, so long as our connection to our spouse doesn't prevent us from moving on in ways that bring us pleasure and happiness.

Sometimes there's a fine line between keeping his memory alive and keeping ourselves stuck. We may hesitate to change our address for fear of betraying our loyalty to all the years we lived under the same roof. We may avoid new relationships, feeling that any show of affection or intimacy pulls us that much farther away. We may table travel plans, career opportunities, even a different hairdo, believing that any and all changes represent breaking ties with our beloved.

But they don't. Even as we move forward, we are sustained by his love. Our foundation is firm; we hold him in our heart and are free to carry on.

AFFIRMATION: I can keep the past while creating my future.

Carrie, widowed just over a year, talks about her reluctance to go forward with her life. "I find myself paralyzed to make new friends, to take a new career position, even to buy new furniture, as if somehow any forward movement symbolizes leaving Barry behind."

But we must move on, with trust and confidence that we have his blessing. In the following space write a letter to your love asking him to release you to life. You might use these words:

My Dearest_____,

I ask your blessing to . . .

*What is resignation? It is putting God between oneself
and one's grief.*

—ANNE SOPHIE SWETCHINE

I prefer the word *surrender* to *resignation;* the first implies a
deep, abiding belief in the unfolding of the cosmos, whereas
the latter sounds like giving up and giving in.

We can be resigned to our circumstances or we can embrace them, with faith that there are reasons, however unknown, for the situation we find ourselves in. Surrender
means that even in the midst of our worst moments we have
confidence in a greater plan. It means we are receptive to the
lessens inherent in this experience. Mostly it means having
faith that no matter how life continues to unfold, we have the
strength and stamina to survive.

AFFIRMATION: I surrender.

Better to be quarreling than lonesome.

—IRISH PROVERB

Hard as it is to believe, we may even miss the squabbling. We may have moaned about it, sick of the arguments and fights, but now conflict would be a welcome reprieve from the loneliness we feel.

Not to mention making up. Those of us whose marriages were sustained over many years may have come to rely fondly on the friendly bickering that we knew didn't amount to a hill of beans. We were used to each other! We miss the security of arguing without worrying about hurt feelings or lasting repercussions.

What we may miss most is the feeling of being emotionally involved and invested. Try not to transfer this need to friends, children, or co-workers. When you feel the urge to engage in combat, restrain yourself. Know that this is just one more loss that gets easier with time.

AFFIRMATION: I even miss the fights.

Without him, the sun will never be as bright.
                                            —RUTH COUGHLIN

Which beautifully sums it up. We have survived our loss, we have learned, and continue to learn, how to go on and live full and meaningful lives despite the ache in our heart.

And we will never forget him. Because indeed nothing is quite as vivid, as sweet, as wonderful as when we were graced by his presence. We are stronger for the experience, more humane for all we have endured.

Without him the sun will never be as bright. But as we gaze toward the infinite reaches of sky, we light on a faraway star and once more say:

AFFIRMATION: Good-bye, my love.

May God bless you and keep you. May her countenance shine upon you. And may you be granted the greatest gift of all. The gift of peace.

—Prayer

I leave you with my favorite prayer. I've been comforted by these words in times of darkness, when I've felt lost and hopeless, unable to summon the strength to go on.

But we must go on. The journey we embarked on one year ago today has brought us to a spiritual crossroads; we have but one one choice—to grow in our strength; to transform our pain into healing, our feelings of loss into a deeper commitment to ourselves, our loved ones, our community, our world.

As you take the next steps on your journey, know that you are blessed. Know that you are safe. Know that your love is eternal, forever tucked beneath the wings of your heart. May you be granted peace. And let us say:

AFFIRMATION: Amen.

INDEX